Greetings From Salem, Massachusetts

Mary L. Martin and
Nathaniel Wolfgang-Price

4880 Lower Valley Road   Atglen, Pennsylvania 19310

Published by Schiffer Publishing Ltd.
4880 Lower Valley Road
Atglen, PA 19310
Phone: (610) 593-1777; Fax: (610) 593-2002
E-mail: Info@schifferbooks.com

Copyright © 2007 by Mary L. Martin & Schiffer Publishing, Ltd.
Library of Congress Control Number: 2007923061

All rights reserved. No part of this work may be reproduced or used in any form or by any means—graphic, electronic, or mechanical, including photocopying or information storage and retrieval systems—without written permission from the publisher.
The scanning, uploading and distribution of this book or any part thereof via the Internet or via any other means without the permission of the publisher is illegal and punishable by law. Please purchase only authorized editions and do not participate in or encourage the electronic piracy of copyrighted materials.
"Schiffer," "Schiffer Publishing Ltd. & Design," and the "Design of pen and ink well" are registered trademarks of Schiffer Publishing Ltd.

Designed by Mark David Bowyer
Type set in Cancun / Souvenir Lt BT

ISBN: 0-7643-2602-3
Printed in China

For the largest selection of fine reference books on this and related subjects, please visit our web site at **www.schifferbooks.com**
We are always looking for people to write books on new and related subjects. If you have an idea for a book please contact us at the above address.

This book may be purchased from the publisher.
Include $3.95 for shipping.
Please try your bookstore first.
You may write for a free catalog.

In Europe, Schiffer books are distributed by
Bushwood Books
6 Marksbury Ave.
Kew Gardens
Surrey TW9 4JF England
Phone: 44 (0) 20 8392-8585; Fax: 44 (0) 20 8392-9876
E-mail: info@bushwoodbooks.co.uk
Website: www.bushwoodbooks.co.uk
Free postage in the U.K., Europe; air mail at cost.

CONTENTS

About Salem 4
   Introduction 4
   History 7
   Salem Witch Trials 13
   Great Salem Fire of 1914 20
   Nathaniel Hawthorne 27
   The House of Seven Gables 30

Inside Salem 36
   Salem Town 36
   Streets 51
   Schools 57
   Churches 61
   Cemeteries 68
   Mills 71
   Houses 73
   Gardens 90
   Salem and the Sea 92

Places to See, Things to Do 96
   Just Visiting 96
   Peabody Essex Museum 100
   Salem Willows 116

Bibliography 126
Index 128

ABOUT SALEM

INTRODUCTION

When most people think of Salem, Massachusetts, they think of the Salem Witch Trials, a regrettable event in American history in which twenty-four innocent people died and many more were imprisoned. However, while the trials played an important part in Salem's history and culture both in the past and in the present, they are not the only thing the city has to offer.

Situated as it was on the East Coast, Salem soon became a haven for the shipping industry with merchant ships from Salem sailing to far-off ports in Asia, Africa, and the East Indies, and returning with ivory, tea, silk, spices, Indian cottons, and other exotic goods. These voyages made the fortunes of many merchants and captains who, in turn, used their money to build stylish and elaborate mansions for themselves and their families, many of which still stand in Salem today preserved as museums and historical sites.

Salem is also the birthplace of Nathaniel Hawthorne, the author of such literary classics as, The House of Seven Gables and The Scarlet Letter. The Hawthorne Hotel and Hawthorne Boulevard bear his name, while several of the sites related to Hawthorne's life in Salem have been preserved as well.

Today, Salem is a thriving tourist destination, attracting visitors from all over the United States and abroad. Even as far back as the 1900s, Salem welcomed visitors with much the same enthusiasm as they once welcomed visiting ship captains and political dignitaries. Visitors to Salem sent back postcards by the dozens enthusiastically describing the places they had been, the sights they had seen, the people they had met, and the good times they were having.

Not just for correspondences, postcards were also a form of early advertising showcasing a city's finest and most interesting assets from historical or modern civic buildings to beautiful natural scenery. Vintage postcards from the 1900s to the 1950s along with historical trivia and quoted material from the backs of the cards will do just that, and showcase some of the sites that have made Salem famous.

Historic Images Through Postcards

Postcards are said to be the most popular collectible history has ever known. The urge to horde them sprang up with the birth of this means of communication at the turn of the twentieth century, and has endured great changes in the printing industry. Today, postcard shows take place every weekend somewhere in the country, or the world, and millions of pieces of ephemera lie in wait for those who collect obscure topics or town views.

Postcards once served as the email of their day. They were the fastest, most popular means of communication beginning in the 1890s in the United States. These timely cards provided a way to send visual scenes through the mail along with brief messages—a way to enchant friends and family with the places travelers visited, to send local scenes, or to share favorite topics of imagery. They even provided the latest breaking news, as images of fires, floods, shipwrecks, and festivals were often available in postcard form within hours of an event. Moreover, mail was delivered to most urban homes in the United States at least twice a day. So someone might send a morning postcard inviting a friend to dinner that evening, and receive an RSVP in time to shop for food.

The messages shared and the beautiful scenes combined to create the timeless appeal of postcards as a collectible. Most importantly, history is recorded by the pictures of the times, moments in time reflecting an alluring past.

Dating Postcards

Pioneer Era (1893-1898): Most pioneer cards in today's collections begin with cards placed on sale at the Columbian Exposition in Chicago on May 1, 1893. These were illustrations on government-printed postal cards and privately-printed souvenir cards. The government cards had the printed one-cent stamp, while souvenir cards required a two-cent adhesive postage stamp to be applied. Writing was not permitted on the address side of the card.

Private Mailing Card Era (1898-1901): On May 19, 1898, private printers were granted permission, by an act of Congress, to print and sell cards that bore the inscription, "Private Mailing Card." A one-cent adhesive stamp was required. A dozen or more American printers began to take postcards seriously. Writing was still not permitted on the back.

Post Card Era—Undivided Back (1901-1907): New U. S. postal regulations on December 24, 1901 stipulated that the words "Post Card" should be printed at the top of the address side of privately printed cards. Government-issued cards were to be designated as "Postal Cards." Writing was still not permitted on the address side. In this era, private citizens began to take black and white photographs and have them printed on paper with postcard backs.

Early Divided Back Era (1907-1914): Postcards with a divided back were permitted in Britain in 1902, but not in the United States until March 1, 1907. The address was to be written on the right side; the left side was for writing messages. Many millions of cards were published in this era.

Up to this point, most postcards were printed in Germany, which was far ahead of the United States in the use of lithographic processes. With the advent of World War I, the supply of postcards for American consumption switched from Germany to England and the United States.

White Border Era (1915-1930): Most U. S. postcards were printed during this period. To save ink, publishers left a clear border around the view, thus these postcards are referred to as "White Border" cards. The relatively high cost of labor, along with inexperience and changes in public taste, resulted in the production of poor quality cards during this period. Furthermore, strong competition in a narrowing market caused many publishers to go out of business.

Linen Era (1930-1944): New printing processes allowed printing on postcards with high rag content that created a textured finish. These cheap cards allowed the use of gaudy dyes for coloring.

Photochrome Era (1945 to date): "Chrome" postcards began to dominate the scene soon after the Union Oil Company placed them in its western service stations in 1939. Mike Roberts pioneered with his "WESCO" cards soon after World War II. Three-dimensional postcards also appeared in this era.

Example of a postcard with an undivided back. Senders could only write the address on this side of the card. Any message needed to be written on the front of the card along with the picture.

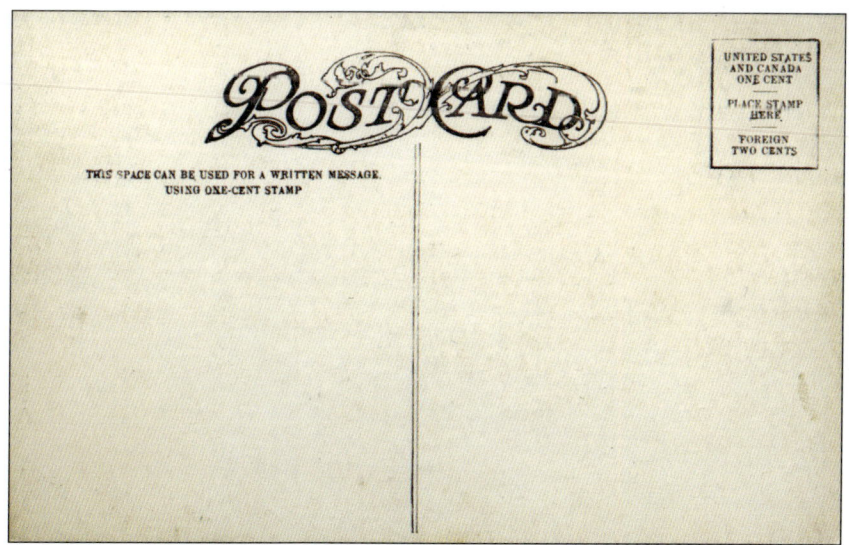

Sample of a postcard with a divided back. Senders were allowed to put an address on the right hand side of the postcard and a message on the left side.

Greetings from Salem, Massachusetts.

Circa 1920s, $2-4

Salem is perhaps best known for the Salem Witch Trials which took place in 1692. Much of the town's culture and tourist industry is based around the trials and those who participated in them.

Cancelled 1907, $3-5

HISTORY

In 1626, Roger Conant and a group of fisherman left rocky Cape Ann and sailed southwest until they reached a cove at the mouth of the Naumkeag River. Conant, who had been nominated to serve as the governor, named his new settlement Naumkeag after the Native American name for the area. In 1628, four hundred settlers from the New England Company, under the leadership of John Endicott, arrived in Naumkeag. The Company had applied for a patent from the English government transferring the ownership rights of Naumkeag to them. The New England Company replaced Conant as governor, appointing Endicott in his place, and renamed the settlement, calling it Salem which means "City of Peace." Endicott continued as governor until 1630 and the arrival of the Winthrop Fleet carrying five hundred settlers, and the charter of the Massachusetts Bay Company, which had replaced the New England Colony. The leader of the fleet, John Winthrop, had already been elected governor of the colony before the fleet had departed England, replaced John Endicott much in the same way he had replaced Conant several years earlier.

Salem's location overlooking Salem Harbor proved to be a great boon to the town. Salem became the focal point for the area around Cape Ann with most of the overseas travel and trade coming to or leaving from Salem at one point in their journey. Colonists and immigrants from England or other parts of New England came to Salem settling in the town, the surrounding area (what would eventually become Salem Village), or moving on to find their own villages. But even Salem's prosperity could not save it from the events that were to come.

From March to January of 1692, hysteria gripped the area around Salem as fear and suspicion drove the people of Salem to accuse neighbors, family, and even complete strangers of being witches. By the end of the Salem Witch Trials, twenty-four people had died and many more had been imprisoned on charges of witchcraft. Even after they ended the events, the trials would effect the culture and history of Salem for many years.

Salem was founded in 1626, by a group of fishermen lead by Roger Conant. The bronze statue of Conant was erected in Salem Common and dedicated on June 17, 1913.

Circa 1920s, $2-4

ROGER CONANT STATUE, SALEM, MASS.

During the American Revolution, Salem joined the rest of the American Colonies in defying the British Crown and fighting the war for independence. With European trade cut off, the merchant ships of Salem turned to privateering, raiding British ships under letters of marque issued by the Continental Congress. On February 16, 1775, Salem Patriots defied the British even further by raising the North Bridge and preventing British troops, under the command of Colonel Alexander Leslie, from crossing the North River and seizing supplies and ammunition hidden in North Salem.

Following the Revolutionary War, Salem returned to the sea, with fishing and trading forming the basis of the city's economy. Merchant trading continued to enrich Salem for many years until the prominence of other ports like Boston and New York caused the shipping industry to decline in the late 1800s. Looking for other sources of income, Salem turned to industry to help fill the void left by the decline of the shipping industry. Soon Salem was home to a number of textile mills, tanneries, and shoe factories. Unfortunately, the factories also brought misfortune to Salem in the form of the Great Salem Fire of 1914, which was caused by a mixture of chemicals overheating and destroying 253 acres of the city. Thankfully, a large portion of Salem's collection of historic buildings survived, which helped Salem develop into the tourism center it is today.

John Winthrop was elected governor of the Massachusetts Bay Colony in 1629. He arrived in Salem in 1630 aboard the *Arabella*.

Circa 1950s, $2-4

The *Arabella* departed England in April of 1630, and landed in Salem in July. It was the flagship of the Winthrop Fleet which consisted of eleven ships carrying 700 settlers, the largest fleet ever assembled to carry English colonists. A replica of the *Arabella* is on display at the Salem Pioneer Village.

Circa 1930s, $3-5

Salem's first settlers came to the area in 1626, led by Roger Conant. A replica of the village (as it would have appeared at the time of Governor Winthrop's arrival) was built in 1930 as part of the Massachusetts Tercentenary Celebration and is still operated as a living history museum.

Circa 1930s, $3-5

A panoramic view of some of the houses of Salem Pioneer Village.

Circa 1930s, $2-4

Many of the houses built in the original Salem village were roofed with thatch made from straw, water reeds, and other locally growing vegetation.

Circa 1930s, $2-4

Many of the early settlers of Salem lived in dugouts or wigwams until more permanent shelters could be built.

Circa 1930s, $2-4

Built in 1628, the Faire House was the home of John Endicott who was appointed governor of the Massachusetts Bay Colony, replacing Roger Conant who had been governor since 1626.

Circa 1930s, $2-4

The early settlers of Salem probably learned how to build wigwams from friendly Native Americans who lived in the area.

Circa 1930s, $2-4

Inside a wigwam. The walls and ceilings were lined with water reeds which acted as insulation keeping heat in and harsh weather out.

Circa 1930s, $2-4

The kitchen of the Faire House.

Circa 1930s, $2-4

The First Meeting House was used for both spiritual and secular meetings. It was built in 1634 and enlarged in 1639. The building was last used for worship meetings in 1670.

Cancelled 1906, $2-4

The First Church in Salem occupied the site of the First Meeting House from 1634 to 1923. Today, a plaque on Essex Street marks where the Meeting House once stood.

Circa 1900s, $2-4

11

To stop British troops from seizing supplies and ammunition stored in the town, patriots from North Salem raised the drawbridge over the North River preventing the British from crossing. This event is commemorated by a marker erected on the site of the old bridge.

Cancelled 1908, $2-4

The 23rd Massachusetts Volunteer Infantry was organized on September 28, 1861. It was made up of ten companies, six from Essex County and one each from Bristol, Worcester, Middlesex, and Plymouth. Two of those companies, A Company and F Company, were raised in Salem.

Circa 1910s, $3-5

To honor the men of the 23rd Massachusetts Volunteer Infantry and the unit's service during the Civil War, a monument was placed in Salem Common on September 28, 1905, on the anniversary of the date the unit was mustered out.

Circa 1900s, $3-5

SALEM WITCH TRIALS

On January 15, 1692, Abigail Williams, the eleven-year-old niece of Samuel Parris, the minister of the church in Salem Village, became very ill. Her cousin Betty, Parris' nine-year-old daughter, soon became ill as well. Eyewitnesses to the girls' illness described it as "beyond the power of any Epileptick Fits or natural Disease to affect." The girls would scream, utter strange sounds, throw things, and complain of being pricked with pins. Parris consulted the village doctor, William Griggs, who could find no natural cause for Betty and Abigail's fits and pronounced that the girls were "under an Evil Hand," meaning they were bewitched.

Inquiries as to the identities of the girls' tormentor (or tormentors) lead to Parris' Carib-Indian slave, Tituba. Traditionally, it is believed that Tituba had entertained Betty and Abigail with stories about Barbados and magic, and as time wore on, actually taught them, and other young girls in the village, tricks of witchcraft and fortune telling. However, there is no contemporary evidence to support this belief.

Further inquiries and other reported afflictions revealed the names of two more witches, Sarah Osborne and Sarah Good. All three fit the stereotypes of an accused witch: all three were outsiders who had not been born in Salem Village, neither Osborne or Good were church members, and both were extremely unpopular with the residents of the village. Additionally, Sarah Good had been accused of witchcraft before, and Sarah Osborne had been involved with a legal dispute with the family of one of her accusers, Ann Putnam.

Additional reports of afflictions resulted in the accusation of other residents of Salem Village including, John and Elizabeth Proctor, Abigail and Deliverance Hobbs, Dorcas Good (Sarah's four-year-old daughter), Rebecca Nurse, and Martha Corey. The last two surprised many people since both Nurse and Corey were respected members of the community—if such pious and respected people could be witches, than anybody could. The widening circle of accusation led to more accusations and arrests until the jails in Salem and the surrounding areas were full of suspected witches.

In May 1692, Sir William Phips arrived in Boston to assume the governorship of the Massachusetts Bay Colony. Surprised to find the jails in Boston and Salem filled with accused witches, he established a Court of Oyer and Terminer (to hear and determine) to process the immense number of witchcraft cases. Phips appointed nine local men, William Stoughton, John Hathorne, Jonathan Corwin, Bartholomew Gedney, Nathaniel Salstonstall, Samuel Sewall, John Richards, Peter Sergeant, and Waitstill Winthrop to serve as judges and councilors who, in turn, sent out a call for eighteen men of good character to serve on the grand jury and forty men of similar character to serve on trial juries. It would be the Court's job to declare judgment and pass sentence on an accused witch after the witch's case had been examined by two or more magistrates and set before the Grand Jury. The Court of Oyer and Terminer officially convened for the first time on June 2, 1692, at the courthouse in Salem Town and continued to process cases against accused witches until October 29, when Governor Phips officially dissolved the Court and forbade the arresting of any more suspects.

By the time the trials had officially ended in January 1693, a total of nineteen people had been found guilty of witchcraft and executed by hanging, four had died in prison awaiting trial or sentencing, and one had been pressed to death for refusing to enter a plea.

The end of the trials brought about a change in consciousness in both Salem Village and Salem Town with many of those involved in the trials expressing regret, and in some cases, publicly apologizing for their roles in the Witchcraft Trials. In 1711, the colony of Massachusetts officially passed a bill restoring the good names and rights of any accused of witchcraft during the trials and granting their heirs £600 restitution. In the 1950s, Massachusetts officially exonerated the accused and formally apologized for the Salem Witch Trials.

Because of the historical and cultural importance attached to the Witch Trials, Salem has been given the nickname, "the Witch City."

Circa 1900s, $5-7

A witch was often served and aided by a familiar, an imp, or similar spirit that would often take the form of an animal like an owl, toad, dog, or cat (particularly black cats). These familiars were believed to be the witch's link to the Devil and derived nourishment from sucking on the witch's body.

Circa 1940s, $3-5

Witches were reputed to possess a number of magical powers including the power to fly using a broom or a distaff (a tool used to keep unspun from getting tangled).

Circa 1900s, $4-6

Witches were also reputed to gather in groups called covens for the purpose of casting spells and creating mischief.

Circa 1900s, $4-6

14

The Shattuck Witch House was built on Essex Street sometime before 1675.

Cancelled 1903, $4-6

Corwin purchased the house, in 1675, from Nathaniel Davenport, a merchant from Boston, and had lived in it for several years prior to the Witchcraft Trials.

Circa 1900s, $3-5

The Witch House was owned by Jonathan Corwin, one of the Salem magistrates who presided over the examination of many of the individuals accused of witchcraft and later served as judge and councilor on the Court of Oyer and Terminer.

Cancelled 1922, $3-5

Despite its name, no witch, or anyone accused of being a witch, had lived or been imprisoned in the Witch's House. At present, it is the only standing structure in Salem that has a direct link with the Salem Witch Trials.

Circa 1920s, $3-5

Jacobs was tried on August 4th, and found guilty of witchcraft. He was hanged on August 19th, one of the first men to be executed for witchcraft in Salem.

Circa 1910s, $3-5

George Jacobs, Sr. was arrested on charges of witchcraft on May 10, 1692. His main accusers were Abigail Williams, his servant, Sarah Churchwell, and his granddaughter, Margaret. Both Sarah and his granddaughter had confessed to being witches and had implicated Jacobs in their confessions.

Circa 1900s, $3-5

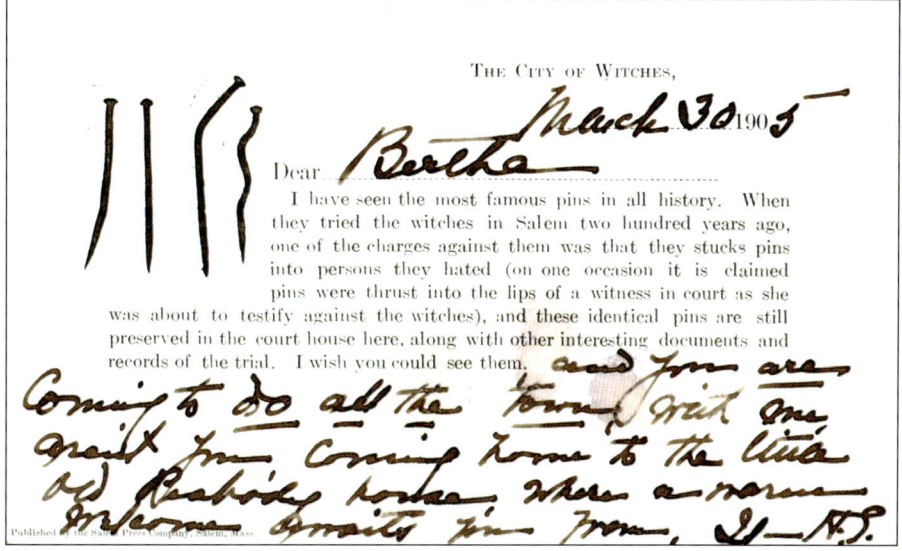

A number of those accused of witchcraft in Salem were said to send their specters to stick pins into the bodies of their accusers. Several pins were entered as evidence during the trials and are on display at the Superior Court Building.

Cancelled 1905, $3-5

During the Salem Witch Trials, those accused of witchcraft were held in the Old Witch Jail. There were no bars or cells, but surprisingly, none of the captives tried to escape.

Circa 1930s, $5-7

The attic of the Old Witch Jail. One man, three women, and several infants died in the Jail during the Witch Trial.

Circa 1930s, $2-4

Under English law, any act of witchcraft or magic that directly or indirectly harmed or killed a person was a capital crime punishable by death.

Circa 1900s, $3-5

The first person to be executed for witchcraft in the Salem Witchcraft Trials was Bridget Bishop, who was also the first to be convicted. She was hanged on June 10th at Gallows Hill.

Circa 1900s, $3-5

Born in Salem on August 5, 1641, John Hathorne served as a Salem magistrate and as a judge and councilor for the Court of Oyer and Terminer. He died on May 10, 1717, and was one of the few people involved in the trial that did not later repent his actions.

Circa 1910s, $1-3

Four sets of executions were held on Gallows Hills between June 10th and September 22nd. Martha Corey, Mary Parker, Margaret Scott, Samuel Wardwell, Ann Pudeator, Alice Parker, and Wilmot Redd were the last accused witches to be hanged on Gallows Hill.

Circa 1920s, $2-4

Using life-sized figures, stage sets, dramatic lighting, and historical narration, the events of the Witch Trials are recreated inside the Salem Witch Museum.

Circa 1960s, $2-4

GREAT SALEM FIRE OF 1914

At 1:37 pm June 25, 1914, a fire alarm box was pulled in Salem's Leather District to report a fire at the Korn Leather Factory on Boston Street. The fire had begun in a storage shed which opened up onto the factory's street floor and was used to store acetone, celluloid, amalacitate, and alcohol, which were being used in the manufacture of tip finish for patent leather.

The fire spread from the factory to the Quinn Block to the east, and the Creedon Factory to the west, crossed Proctor Street, and burned the Cunney Factory, all the while continuing down Boston Street. It quickly grew larger than local authorities could handle and the call for aid was sent out. Additional firefighters were called in from the nearby communities of Beverly, Peabody, Swampscott, Lynn, and Marblehead. Even with the additional help, the fire continued to spread, and it fell to the police department to call for additional aid, ninety policemen from twenty-one different cities and seventeen hundred militiamen answered the Salem Police Department's call. The fire continued to rage throughout the city until it reached Lane's Wharf where the firefighters were able to contain and eventually extinguish the blaze, but not before it had burned across 253 acres and destroyed 1,376 more. Of the 48,000 people living in Salem, 20,000 were left homeless and 10,000 were left jobless.

According to an urban legend, the ghost of Giles Corey was spotted before the fire. Corey had died during the events of the Salem Witch Trials in 1692 by refusing to enter a plea when accused of witchcraft. It is said that his ghost will appear the night before a tragedy will befall the city.

Prior to the fire, attempts had been made by Councilman Franklin H. Wentworth to introduce an order that would require all new or replacement roofs or roof-coverings to be made of non-flammable materials. Wentworth's opponents accused him of only considering the benefits that the order would provide to the insurance industry, and the order was never passed.

Circa 1910s, $9-11

The Great Salem Fire of 1914 started in a shed at the Korn Leather Factory on Boston Street. It was discovered by Rueben Salkovitch, one of the workers at the factory.

Cancelled 1914, $8-10

Another attempt to update Salem's fire safety measures was made by Charles J. Collins who lobbied for high-pressure pumps for the city's fire wagons. He argued that pumps would pay for themselves in the reduction in insurance costs.

Circa 1910s, $9-11

The Point, after the Fire.

Cancelled 1914, $8-10

The Leather District during the Great Salem Fire. The fire was reported from a firebox in this district.

Circa 1910s, $8-10

Typical Salem Residential Street Prey to the Flames, Salem, Mass.

Over a thousand buildings were destroyed in the Great Fire. Of that number, four hundred of those were houses.

Circa 1910s, $8-10

Mill St., looking toward South Salem, after Fire of June 25, 1914.

A view of Mill Street after the fire. The fire caused extensive damage to Salem's mills and factories leaving 10,000 people jobless.

Circa 1910s, $8-10

RUINS ON POND ST., GREAT SALEM FIRE, JUNE 25, 1914.

Ruins on Pond Street. The building codes prior to the Great Salem Fire were fairly outdated making no mention of safety measures like standpipes, fire sprinklers, or fire escapes.

Circa 1910s, $9-11

Arlington Street.

Circa 1910s, $7-9

Prior to the fire, the total assessed value of the properties in Salem was valued at $37.25 million.

Circa 1910s, $7-9

Though they managed to mobilize rather quickly, the Salem fire and police departments' efforts to contain the fire were unsuccessful. Requests for aid were quickly sent out, eliciting the help of over ninety policemen from twenty-one different cities.

Circa 1910s, $7-9

The remains of the Naumkeag Steam Cotton Company, one of the forty-one factories destroyed in the Fire.

Circa 1910s, $6-8

Despite the severity of the fire, there were only a small number of injuries and deaths reported.

Circa 1910s, $6-8

The ruins of the Creedon Factory.

Circa 1910s, $6-8

According to Salem folklore, the ghost of Giles Corey is supposed to appear shortly before a tragedy is to befall the city. An urban legend states that Corey's ghost was sighted in a graveyard before the Fire of 1914.

Circa 1910s, $6-8

St. Joseph's Church after the Fire.

Circa 1910s, $6-8

Refugees on Salem Common. In his arguments to have the roofs in Salem replaced with fire-proof material, Councilman Wentworth warned that after a large fire, many of Salem's working class would be left homeless and sleeping in tents.

Circa 1910s, $5-7

Out of the 48,000 people living in Salem in 1914, 20,000 were left homeless after the Great Fire.

Circa 1910s, $5-7

Some of the household goods rescued from the Great Salem Fire.

Circa 1910s, $4-6

The first call for military assistance went out at 2:31 pm, nearly an hour after the fire was reported. Seventeen hundred militia members were deployed in Salem to keep order after the Fire.

Circa 1910s, $4-6

NATHANIEL HAWTHORNE

Nathaniel Hawthorne was born in Salem, Massachusetts on July 4, 1804, to Captain Nathaniel Hathorne and Elizabeth Clarke Manning. Nathaniel Hawthorne added the "w" to his name when he was in his mid-twenties to avoid association with his infamous ancestor, John Hathorne.

Following his father's death in 1808, Hawthorne along with his mother and sisters, moved to the Manning House, his maternal grandparent's home on Herbert Street. Hawthorne disliked the Manning House intensely and frequently referred to it as "Castle Dismal."

In 1821, at the age of seventeen, Hawthorne was accepted at Bowdoin College in Brunswick, Maine, where he was friends and classmates with Henry Wadsworth Longfellow and future president Franklin Pierce.

Nathaniel Hawthorne returned to Salem following his graduation in 1825, where he once again took up residence in "Castle Dismal" and began writing and publishing sketches and short stories in newspapers and literary magazines. His first book, Fanshawe, was published in 1828. After the publication of his first short story and sketch collection, Twice Told Tales, Hawthorne's work became very popular, and suddenly the young author found himself the guest of honor at a number of gatherings in Salem and Boston. It was at one such gathering that he met Elizabeth Peabody who was also a resident of Salem. Through Elizabeth, he met Sophia Peabody, Elizabeth's younger sister and his future wife. They were wed on July 9, 1842, in Boston. From Boston, Hawthorne and his wife moved to the Old Manse in Concord, Massachusetts where their first child, Una, was born.

In 1845, financial trouble saw the Hawthorne's moving back to Salem to once again take up residence in the Manning House on Herbert Street. Nathaniel Hawthorne's friends among the Democrat Party, many of whom he met while attending Bowdoin, got him a job as a Surveyor for the Port of Salem. Unfortunately, the position did not last long, and Hawthorne lost his job after the presidential election of 1848, when the Whigs defeated the Democrats. After losing his job, Hawthorne threw himself into his writing, finishing The Scarlet Letter in 1850. From Salem, he and his family moved to Lenox, Massachusetts, and then returned to Concord. In 1853, Nathaniel Hawthorne was appointed United States Consul at Liverpool and Manchester, England, a post which he occupied for four years, until concerns regarding Sophia's health and the tumultuous state of United States politics moved him to resign.

After traveling through Europe for three years, the Hawthornes returned to America in 1860. In an effort to regain some of his health, which had begun to fail following a trip south to Washington D.C. in 1862, Hawthorne and his old classmate, Franklin Pierce, embarked on a tour of New England in 1864. Six days into the trip, Nathaniel Hawthorne died in his sleep at the Pemigewasset House in Plymouth, New Hampshire on May 19, 1864.

Today, Nathaniel Hawthorne is remembered as one of Salem, Massachusetts' most famous residents. Several civic features including Hawthorne Avenue and the Hawthorne Hotel bear his name, while many of the buildings relating to his life and work in Salem have been preserved.

The bronze statue of Nathaniel Hawthorne was commissioned by the Hawthorne Memorial Association and dedicated on December 23, 1925.

Circa 1940s, $2-4

Nathaniel Hawthorne was born in Salem on July 4, 1804, the son of Elizabeth Clarke Manning and Nathaniel Hathorne Sr., a descendent of magistrate and witch judge John Hathorne.

Circa 1910s, $3-5

Hawthorne's family moved from this house to the Manning House on Herbert Street in 1808.

Cancelled 1913, $3-5

From 1846 to 1849, Hawthorne worked as a surveyor in the Salem Custom House; he lost his position due to the change of administration in Washington D.C. following the election of 1848. It was the common practice of the time for the victorious political party to award important political positions to their cronies for their support during the election campaign.

Circa 1940s, $3-5

Nathaniel Peabody bought the Grimshawe House in 1835. He lived there with his wife, Elizabeth, and their three daughters Elizabeth, Mary, and Sophia.

Circa 1900s, $3-5

Following his dismissal from the Custom House, Hawthorne retired to his home on Mall Street where he wrote his famous novel, *The Scarlet Letter*.

Circa 1910s, $3-5

During his courtship of Sophia Peabody, Hawthorne became very familiar with the Peabody's house, using it as the setting for two of his works, *Dr. Grimshawe's Secret* and *The Dolliver Romance*.

Cancelled 1921, $3-5

THE HOUSE OF SEVEN GABLES

"Halfway down a by-street of one of our New England towns stands a rusty wooden house, with seven acutely peaked gables, facing towards various points of the compass, and a huge, clustered chimney in the midst. The street in Pyncheon Street; the house is the old Pyncheon House; and an elm-tree, of wide circumference, rooted before the door, is familiar to every town-born child by the title of the Pyncheon Elm."
—Hawthorne, *The House of Seven Gables*

Though he denies it in the preface, the house described by Nathaniel Hawthorne in the preface to his novel, *The House of Seven Gables*, bears a striking resemblance to the old Turner House, also known as the House of Seven Gables, on Turner Street. The original Turner House was a two room, two and a half story house built in 1668 for Captain John Turner. Shortly after it was finished, Captain Turner added a kitchen lean-to on the house's back and an addition containing a parlor and bedroom on its south side in 1680. His son, John Turner II, further added onto the house, building a kitchen ell at the house's rear and a secret staircase inside the main chimney.

The Turner House remained in the Turner family for another generation, until the loss of his family fortune forced John Turner III to sell the house to the Ingersoll family. The Ingersolls were relatives of Nathaniel Hawthorne, who was a frequent visitor to the house as a guest of his cousin, Susannah. Though the house only had four or five gables at the time of his visit, Hawthorne was well aware of its history and had been seen at the location of the old gables in the attic.

In 1908, the Turner House was purchased by Caroline O. Emmerton, who intended the House to be a non-profit museum. The proceeds from the museum would go to support various settlement programs. Emmerton hired Boston architect Joseph Everett Chandler to oversee the house's restoration. Though, for the most part, the restorations are historically accurate, some historic details were sacrificed in order to make the House more closely resemble the house from Hawthorne's novel.

Also known as the Turner-Ingersoll Mansion, the House of Seven Gables was built for Captain John Turner in 1668.

Circa 1940s, $3-5

The House remained in the Turner family for three generations until it was sold to the Ingersolls who were relations of Nathaniel Hawthorne.

Circa 1920s, $4-6

Hawthorne was a frequent guest at the House of Seven Gables visiting his cousin, Susannah. It was her description of the House's appearance in its early days that gave him the inspiration for the title of his novel, *The House of Seven Gables*.

Circa 1910s, $4-6

Another view of the House of Seven Gables' Parlor.

Circa 1920s, $2-4

The parlor of the House of Seven Gables.

Circa 1940s, $2-4

31

While many believe the House of Seven Gables to be the inspiration for the house in Hawthorne's novel, there are some who maintain that the house Hawthorne wrote about was actually the house that belonged to Phillip English.

Circa 1940s, $2-4

The Dining Room of the House of Seven Gables. The entrance to the secret staircase is visible in the far corner.

Circa 1940s, $2-4

The kitchen of the House of Seven Gables.

Circa 1940s, $2-4

Hallway and servant's staircase. The paper on the walls is a reproduction of the wallpaper hung in the house one hundred years ago.

Circa 1920s, $2-4

In *The House of Seven Gables*, one of the main characters, Hepzibah Pyncheon, must run a shop out of her home in order to support herself.

Circa 1920s, $4-6

Hepzibah's shop was one of several features added onto the House of Seven Gables in order to make it more closely resemble the house described in the novel.

Cancelled 1960, $3-5

Phoebe's Room.

Circa 1940s, $2-4

Clifford's Room showing the secret staircase which leads down to the dining room. The staircase was added by John Turner II in 1692.

Circa 1940s, $2-4

Dating back to the late 1600s, the House of Seven Gables is one of the oldest wooden structures in New England.

Circa 1920s, $2-4

Built by John Beckett in 1655, the Retire Beckett House is the oldest house on the House of Seven Gables site. It is named after Retire Beckett, the shipwright who built the Recovery, the first ship to sail to Arabia, and the Mount Vernon, a privateer which outran an entire French fleet.

Circa 1900s, $3-5

Benjamin Hooper built the Hooper-Hathaway House in 1682, on land purchased from Governor John Endicott. It has been claimed that some of the beams in the house's great hall were salvaged from the house built for Governor Endicott.

Circa 1940s, $2-4

In 1911, the Hooper-Hathaway House was moved from Washington Street to its current location at the House of Seven Gables site.

Circa 1910s, $2-4

INSIDE SALEM

SALEM TOWN

First settled in 1626, Salem is the second oldest settlement in New England and the second city in Massachusetts to be incorporated. The first inhabitants of Salem arrived in 1626, with Roger Conant; the first settlers arrived two years later from England. Salem was incorporated as a town, one year after that, in 1629. Salem continued under the town charter until 1836, when a town meeting was called to assess the residents' opinions regarding the possibility of switching from a town government to a city government. At the meeting, it was decided that a committee would be formed in order to reach a definite decision. The committee would be made up of three members of each of the town's wards and would meet with the town's selectmen. The committee reached a decision, in February 1836, to begin the change. Salem's city charter was approved by the state governor and on April 4, 1836, the residents of Salem voting to accept the new City Charter, making the second city in Massachusetts to be incorporated.

In its early days, Salem encompassed most of the North Shore, the suburban area north of Boston along Massachusetts Bay. Over the years, portions of Salem have been set off or annexed to form many of the nearby communities including Danvers, Marblehead, Lynn, Beverly, Manchester, and Topsfield. At present, it encompasses approximately eight square miles in Essex County.

The doorway to the old Custom House.

Cancelled 1909, $2-4

The Custom House, where Hawthorne worked, was the last in a series of Custom Houses built in the city since 1649. The one pictured here was built in 1805.

Circa 1900s, $10-12

City Hall appears in Hawthorne's short story, "The Sister Years," in which 1838 and 1839 meet and talk on the steps of the newly constructed building.

Cancelled 1911, $5-7

Salem City Hall, built in 1838. The money for its construction came from a portion of a $40 million surplus in the United States Treasury which was distributed to various states within the country.

Circa 1920s, $6-8

Salem Superior Court, a number of artifacts relating to the Salem Witch Trials are on display here, including the official Essex County Seal used to stamp trial documents.

Cancelled 1910, $6-8

The Salem Superior Courthouse and the Essex County Commissioners Building.

Cancelled 1915, $6-8

Essex County has two county seats, one in Lawrence and the other in Salem.

Cancelled 1912, $6-8

The Registry of Deeds in Salem contains some of the oldest and most complete county records in the United States. Currently, the Registry is in the midst of a project to restore and protect its many historic documents.

Cancelled 1912, $5-7

On display inside the Probate Courthouse are original transcripts of the Salem Witch Trials along with the death warrant of Bridget Bishop.

Circa 1920s, $6-8

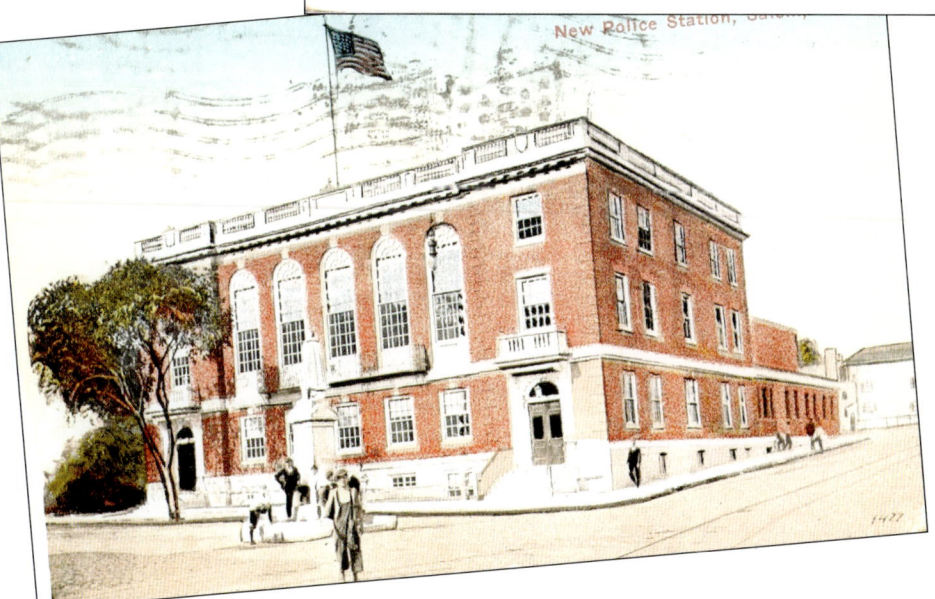

The Salem Police Department was stationed in a building on Front Street from roughly 1865 to 1914, when they moved to a new station on Central Street.

Cancelled 1915, $6-8

Captain John Bertram built the Salem Public Library building in 1855 for use as a private home for him and his family.

Circa 1920s, $5-7

A few years after his death in 1882, Captain Bertram's widow and daughters donated the Library building to the City of Salem for use as a public library.

Circa 1930s, $6-8

The 2nd Corps of Cadets purchased the Essex Street home of Colonel Francis Peabody for use as a head house (the part of the armory where offices and social rooms are located) in 1890.

Circa 1900s, $5-7

In 1908, the Peabody House was demolished and the new State Armory on Essex Street was erected in its place.

Circa 1920s, $7-9

40

In 1838, the Eastern Railroad opened a line which ran from Boston to Salem. The company eventually became a subsidiary of the Boston and Maine Railroad.

Circa 1920s, $7-9

Phenix Hall on Central Street.

Circa 1910s, $6-8

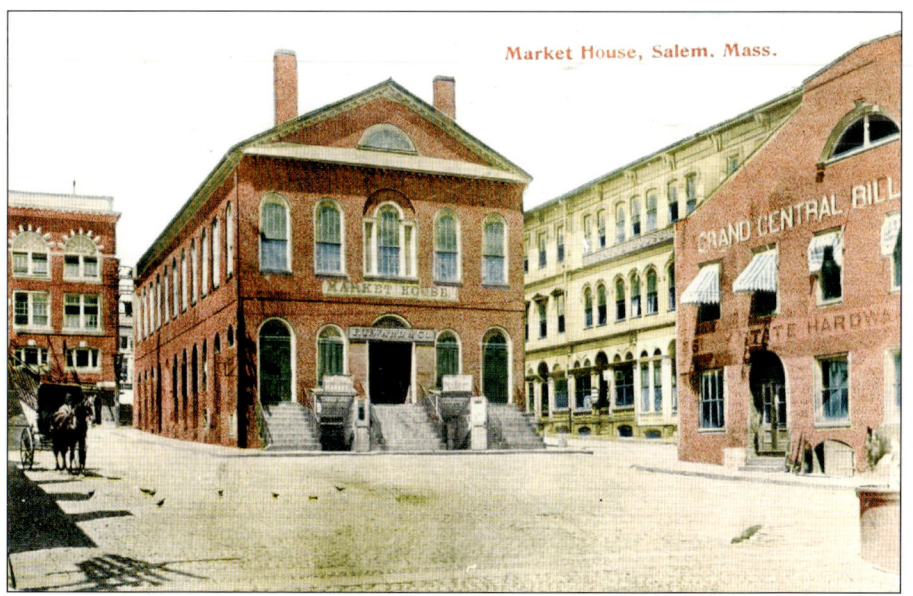

Salem Market House.

Cancelled 1917, $6-8

Fishing was a major industry in Salem going back to its founding in the 1600s. A good portion of what was caught, was sold in places like the Salem Market Place.

Cancelled 1906, $7-9

Organized in 1810, the Salem Athenaeum was one of Salem's first permanent cultural institutions. A number of the city's well-known citizens, like Nathaniel Bowditch and Nathaniel Hawthorne, spent a great deal of time in the Athenaeum borrowing heavily from its collection.

Circa 1920s, $5-7

The entrance to the Salem Club.

Cancelled 1909, $2-4

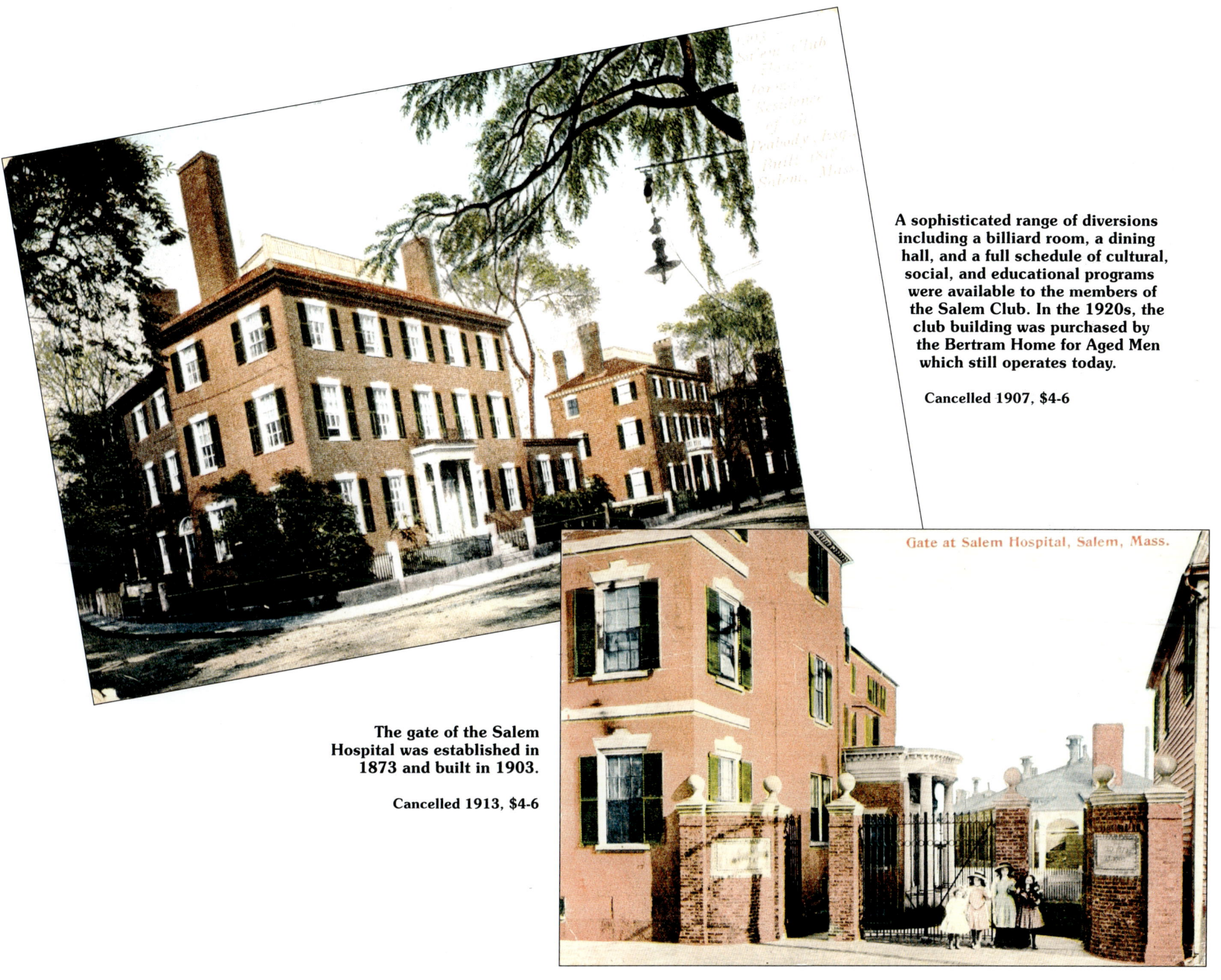

A sophisticated range of diversions including a billiard room, a dining hall, and a full schedule of cultural, social, and educational programs were available to the members of the Salem Club. In the 1920s, the club building was purchased by the Bertram Home for Aged Men which still operates today.

Cancelled 1907, $4-6

The gate of the Salem Hospital was established in 1873 and built in 1903.

Cancelled 1913, $4-6

43

From the back: "The Sisters of Charity began their organized work in caring for orphan children in the house on the corner of Washington and Bridge Streets which was purchased and presented to them by Thomas Looby in 1866. They were incorporated in 1871 under the name of the City Orphan Asylum and erected in 1875 a brick building which with an addition in 1893 constitutes the present commodious Asylum."

Circa 1910s, $3-5

One of Salem's wealthiest citizens, Captain John Bertram, put his fortunes to good use funding and establishing a number of local organizations, including the Salem Hospital, for which he was the primary financial supporter.

Circa 1910s, $4-6

The North Shore Babies Hospital. Even in the 1900s, infants still required special care, and many cities had hospitals set up specifically to care for ailing infants and small children.

Cancelled 1925, $3-5

Captain Bertram was also a lifelong supporter of the Home for Aged Women, now called the Brookehouse for Women, which he founded in 1860.

Circa 1910s, $4-6

Like the Home for Aged Women, the Salem Home for Aged Men was also founded by Captain Bertram.

Circa 1910s, $4-6

Salem Y. M. C. A. Building.

Circa 1900s, $5-7

The Salem Y. W. C. A.

Cancelled 1912, $4-6

A marker on the wall of the Masonic Temple tells the location of the old Salem Courthouse (where many of the accused witches were tried during the Salem Witch Trials) which stood opposite the Temple in the middle of Washington Street.

Circa 1920s, $5-7

Looking down Washington Street from Town House Square.

Circa 1900s, $9-11

The construction of a railroad underneath Washington Street in Town House Square, in 1838, did much to help support Salem's flagging economy by making it easier to move freight to and from the warehouses and factories near the harbor.

Circa 1920s, $9-11

Town House Square and the old First Church Building.

Cancelled 1911, $7-9

In the early days of the city, Salem Common was used as a practice range for individuals training for militia duty and as a grazing pasture for livestock. The latter use was the cause for some concern with the inhabitants of Salem, as unattended animals would sometimes stray and wander loose through the city.

Circa 1900s, $5-7

The main entrance to Salem Common, also called Washington Square. In 1714, the Common was set aside as a military training field.

Circa 1910s, $4-6

Salem Common was also an important gathering place for the people of Salem, hosting parades, parties, sporting events, and other social and cultural gatherings.

Circa 1920s, $6-8

Now a historical district, Washington Square was once the home of a number of Salem's wealthy citizens. Many of the mansions built in Washington Square have been preserved and are still standing today.

Cancelled 1911, $4-6

Salem Common was renamed Washington Square in 1802.

Circa 1930s, $3-5

Daniel & Low Company retail store on the corner of Essex and Washington Streets, one of the largest mail order dealers in gold jewelry and sterling silver.

Circa 1910s, $9-11

The Colonial Dining Room display inside the Daniel Low & Company Retail Store.

Cancelled 1912, $3-5

STREETS

Salem's first streets were laid out in the 1620s, when the town was first settled and incorporated. More streets were developed as Salem Town expanded beyond its original borders.

Today, several of Salem's streets, such as Chestnut, Derby, Lafayette, and Federal Streets, are part of historic districts. Chestnut Street, for example, is part of the McIntire Historic District. During the era when the mercantile trade was prospering in Salem, it was the home of many of the city's merchants and sea captains and is well-known for its large number of Federal Era style townhouses.

Essex Street as seen from Town House Square.

Circa 1920s, $8-10

A view of Essex Street showing part of Salem's retail district.

Circa 1940s, $7-9

The State Armory and the Essex Institute, two of the many famous buildings found on Essex Street.

Circa 1920s, $7-9

Washington Street looking towards the Boston and Main Railroad Station and Town House Square.

Circa 1920s, $8-10

The Corner of Washington and Federal Streets.

Circa 1920s, $6-8

View of Washington Street showing the Hawthorne Building.

Circa 1920s, $8-10

Lafayette Street was once part of South Fields which was home to a large number of farms and country estates.

Circa 1910s, $6-8

Many of the homes on Lafayette Street were destroyed in the Great Salem Fire. Those buildings that remained or were rebuilt are considered an important part of Salem's architectural heritage.

Cancelled 1911, $6-8

During the Great Age of Sail, when Salem was a major shipping port, many of the sea captains and merchants who lived in the city built their homes on Chestnut Street.

Circa 1910s, $7-9

Waiting for a taxi on Chestnut Street.

Circa 1910s, $3-5

Because of its large number of Federal-style houses, Chestnut Street was made into a historical district in 1971. It merged with the Federal Street Area Historic District in 1981 to form the McIntire Historical District.

Circa 1920s, $7-9

54

Another view of Chestnut Street.

Circa 1910s, $6-8

Looking east down Dearborn Street.

Cancelled 1916, $4-6

Dearborn Street circa 1908.

Cancelled 1908, $3-5

Once part of Salem Village, Beverly remains connected to Salem through the Beverly Bridge.

Cancelled 1907, $2-4

Old North Bridge which Salem Patriots raised to prevent British Troops from crossing the North River.

Circa 1930s, $4-6

The opening of the Floating Bridge, in 1803, made travel between Salem and Lynn shorter and less difficult.

Cancelled 1902, $3-5

SCHOOLS

Salem's first school was established in the 1630s. Classes were taught by Reverend John Fisk and were held in his home. In January of 1639, the town chose Edward Norris to replace Fisk as the town's official schoolteacher. Norris was not paid for his efforts, but relied upon the tuition paid by his students' parents or by the town, if the parents could not afford tuition. The school was held in a small thirty by twenty-five foot building near the First Church. On April 5, 1670, the town voted to hire Daniel Epes, Jr. as a grammar schoolmaster and to pay him twenty pounds a year. The residents of Salem were to provide one-third of that sum.

At present, the Salem Public School District consists of seven elementary schools, one elementary and middle school combination, one middle school, and one high school. There are also three private schools and one charter school.

Salem State College was established as the fourth Massachusetts State Normal School in 1854. Originally intended to be a two year teaching college, it began awarding bachelor's degrees and offering a four-year course of study in 1923, and postgraduate studies in 1955. In 1966, residence halls were built on the campus, and the name of the school was changed to Salem State College.

Some of the grammar schools found in Salem.

Circa 1910s, $3-5

The Saltonstall School on Lafayette Street was opened as an elementary school in 1915. It is named after Leverett Saltonstall the first mayor of Salem.

Circa 1920s, $2-4

During the eighteenth and early nineteenth centuries the Phillips family was actively involved in Salem's merchant shipping industry. When the industry declined, they turned their attention to various charitable and political endeavors, including the Phillips School pictured here.

Circa 1910s, $4-6

The façade principale (principal frontage) of the Académie Ste Chrétienne.

Circa 1930s, $4-6

Salem High School.

Cancelled 1908, $4-6

Another view of Salem High School.

Cancelled 1909, $4-6

The State Normal School was founded, in 1854, by the Massachusetts State Legislature as a women's teachers college. The tuition was waived if a student was from Massachusetts and intended to teach in the state's public school system after graduating.

Cancelled 1940, $4-6

In 1921, the Normal School began offering a bachelor's degree and a four-year study program; master's degrees and postgraduate studies were offered in 1955. The School was renamed Salem State College in 1968.

Circa 1920s, $4-6

To gain practical experience, students at the State Normal School would teach classes in the Training Building.

Circa 1920s, $6-8

Saint Joseph School, part of the parish of St. James Church.

Circa 1910s, $5-7

CHURCHES

On Thursday, August 6, 1629, the Puritan settlers of Salem, gathered together forming the First Church of Salem, appointing the Reverends Francis Higginson and Samuel Skelton as the church's pastors. For many years, the First Church remained the most influential religious institution supported by the Puritan authorities of the Massachusetts Bay Colony. Even if they were not church members, the citizens of Salem were still required to support the ministers of the First Church by paying a tax that funded their salaries. The end of the Salem Witch Trials saw the lessening of the Puritan influence on the religious and secular life in Salem and the Massachusetts Colony as a whole, and saw the arrival and revival of other Christian denominations. Salem's Quakers, who had long been persecuted by the ruling Puritans were finally released from their obligations to pay taxes for the support of the ministers of the First Church in 1728, as were the city's Presbyterians and Episcopalians. The Catholic population of Salem, which had always been small, remained disorganized and without a religious leader until 1790, when the town's selectmen granted them permission to gather, and for a priest to come and minister to them.

The members of the South Congregational Church practiced Congregationalist church governance in which a congregation is organized and then worships independent from any centralized church government.

Circa 1910s, $4-6

South Congregational Church. Many of the Puritans who settled Salem, were Congregationalists.

Circa 1910s, $4-6

The pipe organ inside the South Congregational Church was made by the Estey Organ Company of Brattleboro, Vermont.

Cancelled 1908, $4-6

61

The First Baptist Church of Salem was established in 1803, by members of the Baptist Society of Danvers. The current church structure, minus the steeple which was taken down in 1926, was completed in 1806.

Circa 1900s, $5-7

Salem Pentecostal Church on Church Street.

Circa 1910s, $5-7

Erected in 1857 and dedicated in 1858, the Immaculate Conception Church is home to one of the oldest Catholic parishes in the Archdiocese of Boston.

Circa 1910s, $4-6

Originally dedicated as the Wesley Episcopal Church, the Wesley Methodist Episcopal Church (now Wesley United Methodist Church) was finished in 1889. The cornerstone of the church was laid in 1888.

Cancelled 1917, $4-6

Lafayette Street United Methodist Church worshipped in its building on Lafayette Street from 1910 to 1994, when it merged with Wesley United Methodist Church.

Cancelled 1924, $3-5

Saint Peter's Church was established in 1733. Much of the church's early support came from Phillip English, a Salem merchant who had been accused of witchcraft but had escaped from jail and fled to New York.

Circa 1910s, $3-5

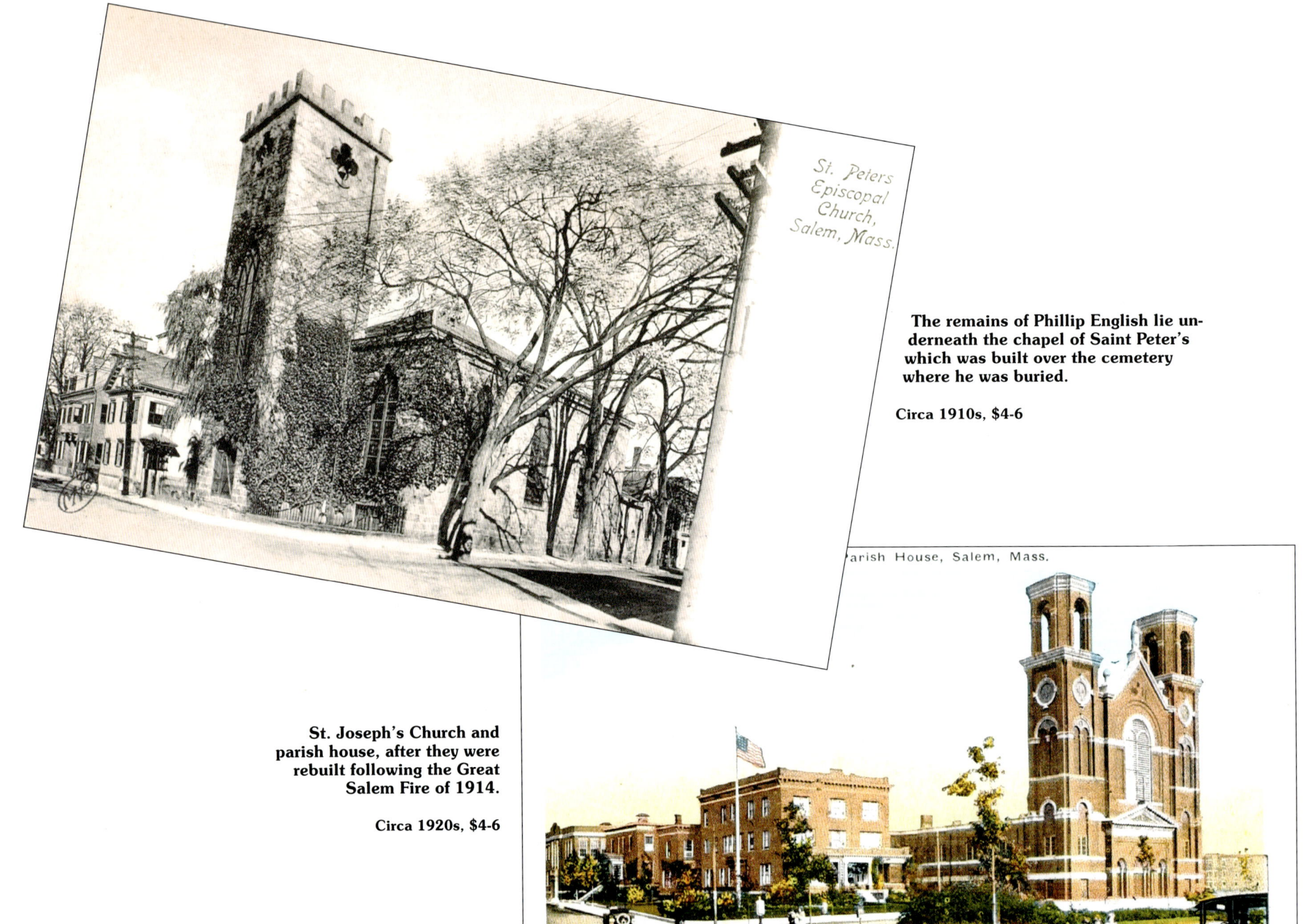

The remains of Phillip English lie underneath the chapel of Saint Peter's which was built over the cemetery where he was buried.

Circa 1910s, $4-6

St. Joseph's Church and parish house, after they were rebuilt following the Great Salem Fire of 1914.

Circa 1920s, $4-6

Located on Route 1-A, Saint Joseph's Church was built in the shape of a cross, a new style in church architecture at the time. Unfortunately, the Church has been closed since August 2004.

Circa 1950s, $3-5

The baldachin (the canopy over the alter) was decorated with twenty-four carat gold-leaf and was dedicated on May 21, 1950.

Circa 1950s, $3-5

The First Church was organized in August of 1692 by the settlers of the Massachusetts Bay Colony and was the first congregational church organized in America.

Circa 1910s, $4-6

The North Church separated from the First Church in 1772. Its second church building was built 1835, and has been the home of the First Church since in merged with the North Church in 1923.

Circa 1910s, $3-5

In 1899, the East Church, which had separated from the First Church in 1719, and the Barton Square Church, which had separated from the First Church in 1824, merged and formed the Second Church. The Second Church merged with the First Church in 1956. The church building is now the home of the Salem Witchcraft Museum.

Circa 1930s, $3-5

Designed by Samuel McIntire, South Church burned down in a fire in 1903.

Circa 1900s, $4-6

CEMETERIES

In 1637, the town of Salem voted to set a portion of land within the town's boundaries for use as a cemetery, choosing a plot of land overlooking the South River. There is some historical evidence that suggests, however, that the plot had already been used as a cemetery long before it was officially designated as one. Salem's oldest, and most famous cemetery, the Burying Point, is the final resting place for the remains of a number of Salem's most famous early citizens and is numbered among Salem's numerous tourist attractions. Salem's other historic cemetery, Greenlawn Cemetery, was opened in 1807, and was, for a time, the principal burying ground of the city. Since 1980, it has been preserved as a park and conservation area.

Soldiers' Monument in Greenlawn Cemetery.

Circa 1910s, $3-5

Opened in 1807, Greenlawn Cemetery was the principal burial ground owned by the city.

Circa 1910s, $2-4

General view of Greenlawn Cemetery.

Cancelled 1910, $2-4

The Greenlawn Cemetery Chapel and Conservatory were given to the city of Salem by the wife of Walter Scott Dickson, in memory of her husband.

Circa 1910s, $4-6

Set aside as a burial ground in 1637, the Burying Point on Charter Street is the oldest cemetery in Salem.

Circa 1910s, $3-5

Gravestones belonging to members of the Lindall family.

Circa 1900s, $2-4

Buried here are a number of historical figures including Richard More, Bartholomew Gedney, John Hathorne, Nathaniel Mather, and Samuel McIntire.

Circa 1920s, $2-4

MILLS

When the shipping industry in Salem began to decline in the late 1800s, the city turned to other forms of industry, manufacturing in particular, to fill the void in their economy. By 1914, a large number of mills, tanneries, and shoe factories had been built in the part of the city known as the Leather District. Perhaps the largest, and most well-known, of these was the Naumkeag Steam Cotton Company, organized in 1839 by Nathaniel Griffin. Known for the quality of the sheeting they manufactured, the company's mills also had the distinction of being the first mills in the country to be run by steam rather than hydro power. The Great Salem Fire of 1914, which originated in the Korn Leather Factory in the Leather District, proved particularly devastating to the manufacturing industry, as many companies lost factories, and many workers lost their jobs. Those companies that did rebuild their factories after the fire, the Naumkeag Company included, stayed in Salem until after the Great Depression when competition from newer factories in the South forced them to move or close permanently.

The Naumkeag Steam Cotton Company's mills were the first in America to use steam power instead of water power.

Circa 1920s, $4-6

The Pope, Phelps, Hackett Mill. From the back: "The miller in 1692 testified that his mill-wheel was unaccountably stopped and 'would not go,' and no reason could be assigned except the demonical malice and power of some witch."

Circa 1910s, $3-5

Following the Great Salem Fire, the Naumkeag Mills were rebuilt using concrete, which the owners hoped would be more fire proof.

Circa 1920s, $4-6

The Naumkeag Mills as seen from Salem Harbor.

Cancelled 1912, $5-7

The Pequot Mills, the home of the famous Pequot brands of sheets and pillowcases.

Circa 1920s, $5-7

HOUSES

Salem is noted for its collection of historical houses, many of which still stand today. Built during the seventeenth, eighteenth, and nineteenth centuries, these houses represent a wide variety of architectural periods and styles ranging from First Period to Georgian Revival. Perhaps the most notable structures in Salem's collection are the Federal-style townhouses designed and built by Samuel McIntire for the merchant aristocracy of Salem.

Some of the houses have since been converted into museums, while others are still maintained as private residences. The Pickering House, for example, has been the home of the Pickering family for ten generations. Still others, have become the headquarters for social service agencies, meeting places for private organizations, and offices for civic institutions. It was the survival of many of these buildings after the Great Salem Fire that allowed Salem to develop as a tourist center.

Today, the majority of Salem's historic houses are located in one of Salem's historic districts: the Derby Historic District (which includes the buildings on Derby Street and extends to Blockhouse Square), the Lafayette Street Historic District (where most of Salem's Victorian houses are located), the McIntire Historic District (which is named after Samuel McIntire and contains most of his surviving works), and the Washington Square District (which contains Salem Common and the houses built around it).

Interior of an old Salem Mansion.

Cancelled 1966, $2-4

Sketch of the Elias Hasket Derby House drawn by Samuel McIntire. Around 1780, Derby hired McIntire to build or remodel houses for Derby's extended family.

Circa 1920s, $3-5

The George M. Whipple House, built in 1804.

Circa 1920s, $3-5

The Poor Estate.

Circa 1910s, $3-5

Pequot House, Salem, Mass.

The Pequot House was built and furnished to resemble the home of a prosperous merchant in the 1650s.

Circa 1920s, $3-5

View of the Pequot House and Pequot Mills in the distance.

Circa 1920s, $3-5

75

Bedroom inside the Pequot House.

Circa 1930s, $2-4

House built by Timothy Lindall. It was later the home of Thomas Barnard, the assistant minister in Andover during the Witch Trials.

Circa 1920s, $3-5

Accused of witchcraft, Phillip English fled to Boston where he was hidden by a friend until he was found and captured. He and his wife, Mary, were held in Boston until around July 1692, when they both escaped to New York. When English returned to Salem a year later, he found his house ransacked and his property seized by the Crown.

Circa 1920s, $3-5

Built around 1651, the Pickering House has been the home of the Pickering family for ten generations. It is the oldest house in the country, continuously occupied by one family.

Circa 1920s, $3-5

John Pickering, Sr. built the Pickering House on land that was granted to him in 1637. His son, John II, and his descendent, Deacon Timothy Pickering, both added onto the original structure, giving the house the appearance it has today.

Circa 1940s, $3-5

The Nicholas Crosby House.

Circa 1920s, $3-5

Simon Bradstreet was the governor of the Massachusetts Bay Colony from 1679 to 1686 and from 1692 to 1697. He lived in the Emmanuel Downing House from 1676 until his death in 1697.

Circa 1920s, $3-5

The Cabot-Endicott House was built in 1744 for merchant Joseph Cabot.

Circa 1920s, $3-5

NO. 3 JOSEPH CABOT HOUSE, SALEM, 1748, DESIGNED BY AN ENGLISH ARCHITECT

The house was eventually bought by William Crownshield Endicott, a Massachusetts Supreme Court Justice who served as Secretary of War under President Grover Cleveland.

Circa 1920s, $3-5

NO. 11 CAPTAIN JONATHAN HODGES HOUSE, SALEM, 1804

This house was built as a double house for Captain Jonathan Hodges in 1804. J. Willard Peele bought the house in 1845, and remodeled the interior to make it a single house.

Circa 1920s, $3-5

Fireplace inside the Cabot-Endicott House.

Circa 1920s, $2-4

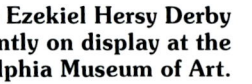

House built for Ezekiel Hersey Derby in 1799. It was designed by Charles Bulfinch.

Circa 1920s, $3-5

A room from the Ezekiel Hersy Derby House currently on display at the Philadelphia Museum of Art.

Circa 1930s, $2-4

The Cook-Oliver House was built by Samuel McIntire for Captain Samuel Cook in 1802-3.

Circa 1920s, $2-4

Captain Richard Derby built the Derby House as a wedding present for his son, Elias Hasket Derby, in 1762. Part of the Salem Maritime National Historic Site, it is the oldest surviving brick house in the city.

Circa 1920s, $3-5

Residence of Judge Joseph Story, an Associate Justice of the United States Supreme Court, and the birthplace of his son, William Wetmore Story, a noted sculptor, poet, and editor.

Circa 1910s, $4-6

Captain Cook's son-in-law, Henry K. Oliver, composed a hymn entitled, "Federal Street," while living with his family in the Cook-Oliver House.

Circa 1930s, $4-6

The Hosmer-Townsend-Waters House on Washington Square.

Circa 1920s, $2-4

Doorway of the John Forrester House.

Circa 1930s, $2-4

The Bowdoin House.

Circa 1920s, $2-4

The Dudley Woodbridge House, which was built around 1786.

Circa 1920s, $2-4

Pineapple Doorway on Brown Street. Many of Salem's homes, especially those built during the 1700s, were decorated with mementos of ocean voyages and faraway lands.

Circa 1920s, $2-4

Leverett Saltonstall I moved to Salem and began his law practice there in 1805. In 1836, he was the first mayor elected in the city of Salem.

Circa 1920s, $2-4

The Whipple House's Old Dutch Door. A Dutch door is a door that is divided in half horizontally and is set up in such a way that top half can be open while the bottom half is still shut.

Cancelled 1910, $2-4

Lee Mansion on Chestnut Street, one of the oldest examples of Greek Revival architecture in Salem.

Circa 1910s, $2-4

West Doorway.

Circa 1920s, $2-4

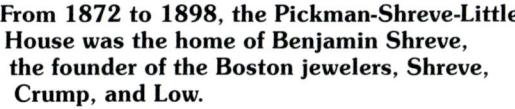

From 1872 to 1898, the Pickman-Shreve-Little House was the home of Benjamin Shreve, the founder of the Boston jewelers, Shreve, Crump, and Low.

Circa 1940s, $2-4

The porch of the Shreve House.

Circa 1930s, $2-4

85

A Salem doorway.

Circa 1920s, $2-4

One of Salem's many Federal-style doorways.

Circa 1930s, $2-4

Gateway to the Emerton House, built in 1820 and designed by Samuel McIntire.

Circa 1930s, $2-4

Doorway on Pickering and Broad Streets.

Circa 1930s, $2-4

Another Salem doorway.

Circa 1910s, $2-4

87

Doorway to the Tucker Rice House, built in 1800.

Cancelled 1920, $2-4

Many of Salem's historic Federal-style houses can be found in the McIntire Historic District.

Circa 1940s, $2-4

Doorway to a house on Chestnut Street.

Circa 1940s, $2-4

The John Albion Andrew House as seen from the house's garden.

Circa 1920s, $2-4

Doorway to the J. Howard Fallen House.

Circa 1920s, $2-4

GARDENS

The first gardens grown in Salem were planted by early settlers for food and for decoration. Any produce that was not mass cultivated or could be gathered locally, was grown in private gardens and used to supplement the household's diet, while flowers and shrubs imported from England or transplanted from the surrounding countryside added color and fragrance to the property it was grown upon. As time progressed and Salem became more settled, gardens were planted more for decoration than any other purpose. Like the houses they surrounded, the gardens of Salem were often viewed as status symbols by Salem's elite. Large and elaborate decorative gardens were tangible examples of prosperity, since only those with a significant amount of money could afford to maintain, or hire people to maintain, a purely decorative garden. As a result, many of the historic homes in Salem feature gardens on their property.

As a young girl, Elizabeth Peabody recalled watching "a little boy with clustering locks" playing in the back garden of the Manning House. Little did she know that the little boy was Nathaniel Hawthorne, her future brother-in-law.

Cancelled 1912, $1-3

View of the Nichols House garden, showing the oldest mulberry tree in New England.

Cancelled 1911, $1-3

Low Estate gardens.

Circa 1910s, $1-3

The oldest tulip tree in New England could be found in the Salem Club garden. Both the Salem Club house and garden were purchased by the Bertram Home for Aged Men in the 1920s.

Circa 1910s, $1-3

The Osgood Hydrangea Garden.

Cancelled 1911, $1-3

The gardens on the grounds of the Old Lord Estate.

Circa 1910s, $1-3

Many of Salem's wealthy families had ornamental gardens attached to their homes. These gardens were often stocked with exotic flora brought back by merchant ships.

Circa 1940s, $3-5

SALEM AND THE SEA

Like many coastal towns, the ocean had a large influence on many of the aspects of Salem. As early as the 1630s, merchants from Salem were involved in trade with the West Indies, trading salted cod for sugar and molasses.

During the Revolutionary War, the focus of Salem's maritime activities shifted from trading to privateering. In order to supplement the small American navy, the Continental Congress distributed letters of marque to commercial ships, granting them permission to attack and capture British ships. Safer and more enjoyable than serving in the army or navy, privateering soon became the most popular form of patriotic service for the citizens of Salem. Oddly enough, it was not very profitable, and only a few merchants retained or maintained their fortunes through the war. Following the Revolution, Salem returned to the mercantile trade expanding their routes to include Africa, the East Indies, and the Far East bringing home cargoes of silk, tea, wine, Indian cotton, and spices. The expansion of the trade routes brought prosperity to Salem, and the city and its people thrived. Shipbuilders received handsome contracts to build larger, faster, and better ships while merchants and ship captains grew rich on the profits brought back by their vessels. The influence of this period of prosperity can be seen even today in the surviving mansions and townhouses built by those same wealthy merchants and in Salem's official motto, Divitus Indiae usque ad ultimum sinum, which means, "To the farthest port of the rich East."

Unfortunately, Salem's golden age did not last, as its harbor was soon eclipsed by the larger ports of Boston and New York, and the merchant trade fell into decline in the late 1800s.

The Norseman, named after the ancient people of Scandinavia, who were famous for their sailing and navigational abilities.

Cancelled 1907, $3-5

Records of Baker's Island date back to 1631, when the island was claimed by Governor John Winthrop and the Commonwealth of Massachusetts. It is not clear, however, how and when Baker's Island got its name.

Cancelled 1907, $2-4

In response to complaints by local mariners that Baker's Island and the waters around it were a navigational hazard, a fifty-seven-foot-tall warning beacon was erected on the island in 1791.

Cancelled 1905, $2-4

The warning beacon was eventually replaced by a pair of lighthouses nicknamed Ma and Pa Baker.

Circa 1900s, $8-10

Both lighthouses and the keeper's cottage were built on land put aside by the federal government.

Circa 1910s, $8-10

Looking east toward the Winter Island Light.

Cancelled 1909, $8-10

Since 1643, Winter Island has been the home of one of Salem's oldest forts. Occupied during the War of 1812, the Spanish-American War, and the Civil War, the fort was given its current name, Fort Pickering, in 1799.

Cancelled 1908, $3-5

Much of Salem's early prosperity came from the shipping trade with Salem merchants trading with ports in the Indies, Africa, and Asia.

Circa 1900s, $3-5

Built by the Salem shipyards by Retire Beckett, *Cleopatra's Barge* was the first ocean-going yacht built in America. The ship only made one transatlantic voyage before its owner, George Crownshield Jr., died on board.

Circa 1920s, $3-5

Dating back 1762, Derby Warf was built by the Derby family, one of Salem's prominent and wealthiest merchant families. During the Revolutionary War and the War of 1812, Derby Wharf was used as a base for privateers operating out of Salem.

Circa 1940s, $4-6

Tar was especially important to Salem, since it was used to seal wooden boats and waterproof sails.

Cancelled 1906, $3-5

PLACES TO SEE, THINGS TO DO

JUST VISITING

Salem's historical and cultural significance have combined to make it a natural destination for visitors. During the golden age of trading, Salem enthusiastically welcomed visiting captains and merchants looking to conduct business with one of the city's merchant families. Political and intellectual notables traveled to Salem at the invitation of the city's elite, or stopped there while traveling their campaign trail.

Tourism, as it is known today, however, started to develop in 1838, with the arrival of the Boston and Maine Railroad. With travel to and from Salem easier and more affordable, the city soon became a popular visitor destination with hundreds of people arriving each day. Salem's tourism industry gained further encouragement in 1925, with the completion of the Hawthorne Hotel, the city's first modern hotel, named after one its most famous residents. In the 1950s, organizations, like Historic Salem Inc., began lobbying for changes to the city's urban renewal plan to preserve the historical buildings that would eventually become an integral part of its growing tourist industry. Today, tourism, along with higher education and health care, is one of the three major industries in Salem.

Burgess Point, as seen from the grounds of the Hotel Fairfax.

Cancelled 1911, $3-5

The Hotel Lincoln on Lafayette Street.

Circa 1940s, $6-8

The Hawthorne Hotel was built in 1925, and designed by Smith and Walker, an architectural firm from Boston.

Circa 1930s, $5-7

Named after Nathaniel Hawthorne, the Hawthorne Hotel is located only a few blocks from the former location of Hawthorne's Union Street birthplace and from 10 Herbert Street, where the author lived with his mother, his sisters, and his extended family on his mother's side.

Circa 1920s, $5-7

There was dancing every night at the North Shore Garden. Admission on Saturdays and holidays cost forty cents for ladies and sixty cents for gentlemen.

Cancelled 1940, $5-7

The J. C. B. Smith Memorial Swimming Pool, the largest open air swimming pool on the East Coast.

Circa 1930s, $4-6

98

An aerial view of the J. C. B. Smith Memorial Swimming Pool.

Circa 1940s, $4-6

Stromberg's at Beverly Bridge, "A Fine Place to Eat."

Circa 1940s, $6-8

Canoeing on the Forest River near Salem.

Cancelled 1914, $2-4

99

PEABODY ESSEX MUSEUM

Exotic cargoes from distant ports were not the only things merchant ships brought to Salem, sailors and captains would often come home with trinkets and other curiosities they had found or purchased on their journeys. Frequently, these objects would find their way into the collection of the East India Marine Society. Open only to captains or supercargoes who had sailed around the Cape of Good Hope or Cape Horn, one of the purposes of the Society was to form a museum of "natural and artificial curiosities," particularly any such items found beyond the two capes. By 1824, the East India Marine Society had accumulated nearly 3,000 items. To house its collection, which had outgrown its old quarters in the Salem Bank Building on Essex Street, the Society built the East India Marine Hall in 1825.

In 1848, the Essex Historical Society merged with the Essex County Natural History Society, forming the Essex Institute. Before the merger, the Essex Historical Society had met on the second floor of Plummer Hall, the former home of the Salem Athenaeum, with its purpose being the collection and preservation of objects relating to the natural, civil, and ecclesiastical history of Essex County.

In 1992, the Peabody Museum (East India Marine Hall) joined forces with the Essex Institute creating the Peabody Essex Museum. The oldest continually-operating museum in the United States, the Peabody Essex Museum is home to a collection of 2.4 million pieces of art and culture, including the original collections from the East India Marine Hall and the Essex Institute. The museum also owns twenty-four historic houses and gardens, all of which are open to the public.

Construction on the East India Marine Hall was completed in October 1825, and was dedicated on October 14th. Attendees of the dedication ceremony included President John Quincy Adams, Judge Joseph Story, Harvard President John Thornton Kirkland, Boston Mayor Josiah Quincy, and Colonel Timothy Pickering of the Pickering House.

Circa 1920s, $5-7

The East India Marine Society was organized, in 1799, for the purpose of sharing navigational information relating to the East Indies, provide support for the disabled members of the society and for the families of deceased members, and to form a museum for the exhibition of "natural and artificial curiosities."

Circa 1920s, $3-5

Membership in the East India Marine Society was open only to ships' masters or supercargoes, an officer on a merchant ship in charge of the cargo, and the business dealings for the voyage, who had sailed around the Cape of Good Hope or Cape Horn.

Circa 1920s, $3-5

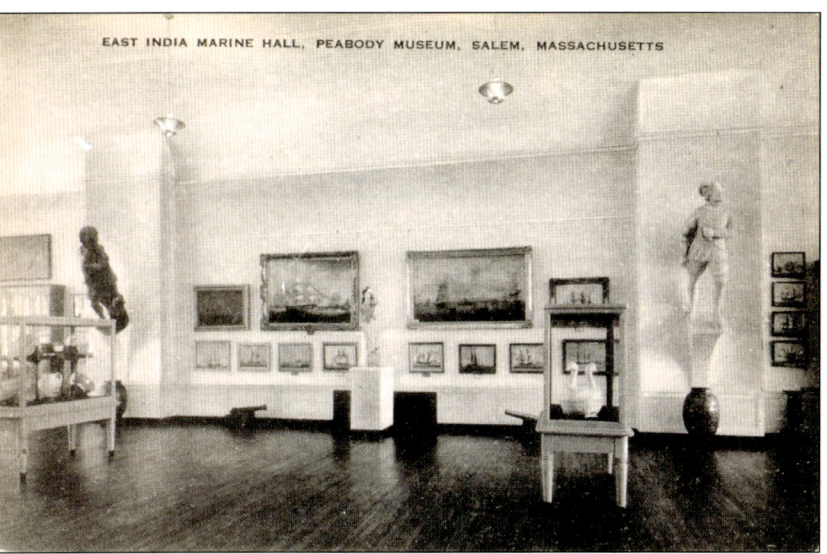

Before being moved to the East India Marine Hall, the Society's collection was housed in rooms in the Sterns Block on Town House Square and in the Salem Bank Building on Essex Street.

Circa 1930s, $2-4

By 1824, the collection owned by the East India Marine Society numbered close to 3,000 pieces. To house its growing collection, the Society organized a corporation for the purpose of financing and constructing a larger building to house the growing collection, the future East India Marine Hall.

Circa 1930s, $3-5

Some of the natural and artificial curiosities exhibited in the East India Marine Hall.

Circa 1930s, $2-4

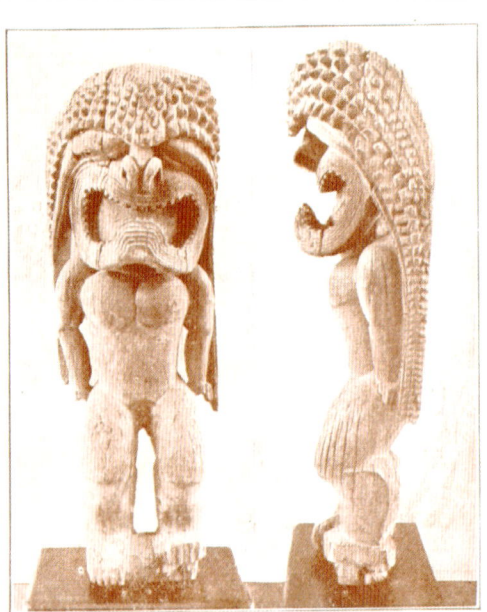

Hawaiian idol carved from "ohia" wood. One of the three surviving images is six-feet-tall and guards the sacrifices in an open-air temple on the island of Hawaii.

Circa 1900s, $2-4

Portrait of Captain Nathaniel Bowditch painted by Charles Osgood. The author of *The New American Practical Navigator*, Captain Bowditch is credited as the founder of modern maritime navigation.

Circa 1930s, $2-4

The terminal bead of a sixteenth century Flemish rosary. The carvings in the bead depict Heaven and the Day of Judgment.

Circa 1930s, $2-4

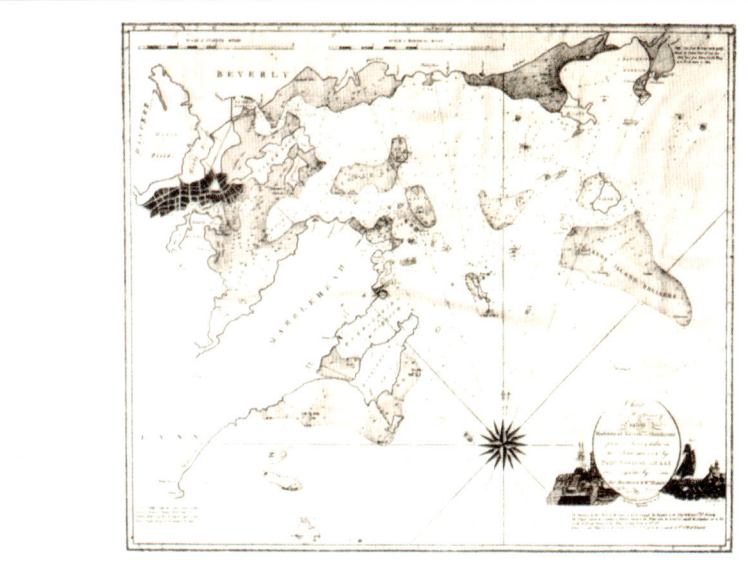

Navigational map of Salem, Beverly, Marblehead, and Manchester harbors published by Captain Bowditch in 1805.

Circa 1930s, $2-4

The Essex Institute was formed in 1848, when the Essex Historical Society merged with the Essex County Natural Society.

Cancelled 1911, $4-6

The Launching of the Ship *Fame* by George Ropes, one of the earliest views of Salem Harbor.

Circa 1950s, $4-6

Essex Institute Picture Gallery.

Circa 1920s, $3-5

On February 26, 1775, Salem Patriots raised the North Bridge halting the advance of troops under the command of Colonel Alexander Leslie, preventing them from seizing supplies stored in North Salem. The event is shown here in the painting, Repulse of Leslie at the North Bridge, on display in the Essex Institute.

Circa 1920s, $3-5

Nineteenth century toys from the Essex Institute's Toy House collection.

Circa 1930s, $2-4

More nineteenth century toys from the Essex Institute's Toy House collection.

Circa 1930s, $5-7

Before the advent of large manufacturers, items of clothing like shoes were often made by hand.

Circa 1920s, $3-5

The parlor was a much more formal room and was used for social gatherings and entertaining guests.

Cancelled 1924, $2-4

Often the warmest room in the house, the colonial-era kitchen was a gathering place for the family during the winter months.

Circa 1920s, $2-4

A New England bedroom, circa 1800.

Circa 1920s, $2-4

Before merging with the Essex County Natural History Society, the Essex Historical Society met on the second floor of Plummer Hall.

Circa 1920s, $2-4

Stairway and pineapple door inside the Essex Institute.

Circa 1920s, $2-4

The Gardner-Pingree House was designed in 1804 by Samuel McIntire, and built by John Gardner, the nephew of Elias Hasket "King" Derby.

Circa 1910s, $2-4

Captain Joseph White, a merchant specializing in trade with the East Indies, purchased the Gardner-Pingree House in 1814.

Circa 1920s, $3-5

On April 7, 1830, Captain White was found brutally murdered in his bed. Four people were arrested in connection with the murder. The hunt for the murderers ended with the arrest of four members of two of Salem's respected merchant families, the Knapps and the Crownshields. One of the Knapps, believing that his wife would inherit Captain White's fortune should he die without a will, hired the two Crownshields to murder the merchant and dispose of his will.

Circa 1930s, $2-4

The trial of Captain White's murderers was followed closely by many of the inhabitants of Salem, including Nathaniel Hawthorne, who used some of the elements of the events in *The House of Seven Gables*.

Circa 1930s, $2-4

The William Crownshield Endicott Memorial Parlours inside the Gardner-Pingree House.

Circa 1930s, $2-4

The Gardner-Pingree House's dining room.

Circa 1930s, $2-4

The Gardner-Pingree House was placed on the National Register of Historic Places in 1970, and is now part of the Peabody Essex Museum's architecture collection.

Circa 1930s, $2-4

Fleeing the plague in England, John Ward came to Salem in 1660. He purchased land and built a house on it in 1684.

Circa 1930s, $3-5

At the time of its construction in 1819, the Andrew Safford House was the most expensive house built in the United States.

Circa 1920s, $2-4

In 1910, the John Ward House was moved from its original location on Peter Street to Brown Street by the Essex Institute, one of the first buildings to be relocated and restored for historic study in the United States.

Circa 1920s, $3-5

Both the interior and the exterior of the John Ward House were restored in order to give visitors an idea of what living conditions were like in Salem in the late 1600s.

Circa 1920s, $2-4

Much like the modern pharmacist, an apothecary was a medical practitioner who mixed and sold medicines to physicians, surgeons, and patients. Apothecaries operated out of a pharmacy-like shop where they sold medicine ingredients, mixed and patent medicines, tobacco, and other dry goods.

Circa 1920s, $2-4

Reproduction of an 1830 cent shop in the lean-to at the rear of the John Ward House.

Circa 1920s, $2-4

Funds for the construction of the Assembly House were raised by selling stock in the building with close to twenty people buying sixty shares. The building itself was built in 1782 to replace the old Assembly Hall on Cambridge Street.

Circa 1930s, $2-4

The Peirce-Nichols House was built for Jerathmiel Peirce on Federal Street in 1782.

Circa 1920s, $2-4

The Assembly House was the site of many functions and entertainments including dances, concerts, and plays. George Washington was the guest of honor at such a function during his visit to Salem in 1789.

Cancelled 1908, $3-5

Peirce was co-owner of the merchant ship, Friendship; part of the Peirce-Nichols House's original property extended to the North River where Peirce could dock his ship on his own property.

Circa 1920s, $3-5

The interior of the Peirce-Nichols House was remodeled in 1810 for the wedding of Sally Peirce and George Nichols.

Circa 1930s, $2-4

Built in 1719 for Samuel Barnard, the Ropes Mansion was purchased by Judge Nathaniel Ropes, Jr., in 1768.

Circa 1930s, $3-5

Three generations of the Ropes family lived in the Ropes Mansion until 1907, when it was given to the Trustees of the Ropes Memorial to use for the benefit of the public.

Circa 1930s, $3-5

The interior of the Ropes Mansion was remodeled by Elizabeth Ropes in 1807.

Circa 1930s, $2-4

The mansion's interior was remodeled again in 1894 in the Colonial Revival style by Mary Pickman and Eliza Orne Ropes.

Circa 1930s, $2-4

The parlor inside the Ropes Mansion.

Circa 1930s, $2-4

Grandfather clocks, like the one on display in the Ropes Mansion, came in two types, thirty-hour clocks and eight-day clocks. Thirty-hour clocks needed to be wound every day, while eight-day clocks were generally more expensive and only needed to be wound once a week.

Circa 1930s, $2-4

All of the furniture inside the Ropes Mansion is original to the property, having belonged to the Ropes family while they still lived in the house.

Circa 1930s, $2-4

The Judge's Chamber, which was once used by Judge Nathaniel Ropes, Jr.

Circa 1930s, $2-4

Located at the rear of the mansion on Essex Street, the Ropes Garden is open to public.

Circa 1930s, $1-3

The Ropes Garden was designed and laid out in Colonial Revival style by John Robinson and added to the Ropes Mansion property in 1912.

Circa 1930s, $1-3

115

SALEM WILLOWS

Named after the European white willow trees planted when its grounds were part of a contagious disease hospital, Salem Willows was designated an official city park in 1858. Like many amusement parks built in the late 1800s, Salem Willows had its beginnings as the enterprise of a local transportation company. The Naumkeag Street Railway Company had been running street cars to the park since 1877, and had been purchasing land for an amusement park for quite some time.

Salem Willows Park officially opened on June 10, 1880. The park was an immediate hit with the community with numerous attractions including a water chute, steamboat cruises around Salem Harbor; Brown's Flying Horses, a merry-go-round (which remained a fixture of the park for nearly seventy years), and the Willow's Pavilion, which featured a roller rink on the first floor and a three-hundred-seat restaurant on the second. Fresh seafood dinners could be found on Ebsen's or Chase's Willow House on Restaurant Row while "traditional" amusement park fare like popcorn, pretzels, and ice cream could be found at Hobbs and Eaton's concession stand at the carousel building. Daily performances by John S. Moulton's opera company or the Salem Cadet Band could be found at Willows Park Theater. For visitors who wanted to stay at the park for more than a day, a tenting ground was set up in the mid 1800s. By the 1900s, the tenting ground had grown into a year-round neighborhood, complete with summer cottages and a hotel, the Juniper Point Inn.

Today, Salem Willows remains open and popular with both residents of Salem and the North Shore, one of the city's most valued treasures.

Salem Willows, an amusement park located at the eastern end of the city near the mouth of Salem Harbor.

Circa 1900s, $1-3

When the park opened in 1880, a column was run in the Salem Evening News to keep the public informed of the happenings in the park. According to the column, nearly 10,000 people visited Salem Willows in one day.

Circa 1910s, $1-3

The Salem Cadet Band, led by Jean Missud, performed regularly at Salem Willows Park, but were only allowed to play sacred music if they gave a concert on a Sunday.

Circa 1910s, $2-4

Under the willow trees in Salem Willows.

Circa 1910s, $1-3

Salem Willows was named for the European white willow trees that were planted to make a shaded walk for patients staying at the hospital that was once located on the park's grounds.

Cancelled 1912, $1-3

For many residents of Salem, a trip to Salem Willows was a sure sign that spring had finally come.

Circa 1930s, $1-3

View of Salem Willows; the town of Beverly is visible in the distance.

Cancelled 1910, $1-3

Crowds of park-goers gather near the Salem Willows boat landing.

Cancelled 1917, $2-4

Built in the 1740s, Fort Lee was intended to protect Salem and Salem Harbor against naval attacks.

Circa 1910s, $1-3

Visitors to Salem Willows could purchase a ticket for a steamer cruise around the harbor.

Circa 1910s, $4-6

The motor boat landing.

Circa 1910s, $3-5

The Salem Willows Yacht Club.

Circa 1940s, $2-4

If they so chose, visitors could also charter a private harbor excursion or join a fishing party at the pier.

Circa 1930s, $2-4

Abbott Cove.

Circa 1910s, $2-4

119

Salem Harbor as seen from Salem Willows.

Cancelled 1913, $3-5

In the eighteenth and nineteenth century, it was not uncommon for men and women to sea bathe separately in order to preserve modesty. However, by the twentieth century, rules regarding public bathing had become more relaxed, and men and women were often seen swimming in the ocean together.

Circa 1920s, $2-4

The Beach at Salem Willows. Sea bathing, swimming in the ocean or in sea water, was especially popular during the late 1800s and early 1900s, with many seaside towns setting aside beaches for public bathing.

Circa 1900s, $2-4

A seawall, like the one pictured here, is built along a beach to prevent erosion and to protect any nearby buildings from high waves.

Circa 1910s, $4-6

One of the main attractions in Salem Willows was the Willows Pavilion which featured a roller skating rink, complete with live music and a restaurant capable of up to three hundred people.

Circa 1900s, $4-6

Ebsen's Willow's House, "famous the country over for its lobster, chicken and steak dinners."

Circa 1950s, $6-8

Salem Willow's famous Restaurant Row.

Circa 1930s, $6-8

121

SWENBECK'S—SALEM WILLOWS, ON THE OCEAN FRONT. 5 MINUTES FROM SALEM COMMON

SWENBECK'S LOBSTER AND FISH DINNERS.

Swenbeck's was known "coast to coast" for its famous lobster and fish dinners.

Circa 1920s, $5-7

Chase's Willow House, opened in 1874.

Circa 1920s, $6-8

Juniper Point began as a tenting ground in the mid 1800s and has since grown into a year-round residential neighborhood.

Circa 1940s, $5-7

The west side of Juniper Point.

Circa 1910s, $4-6

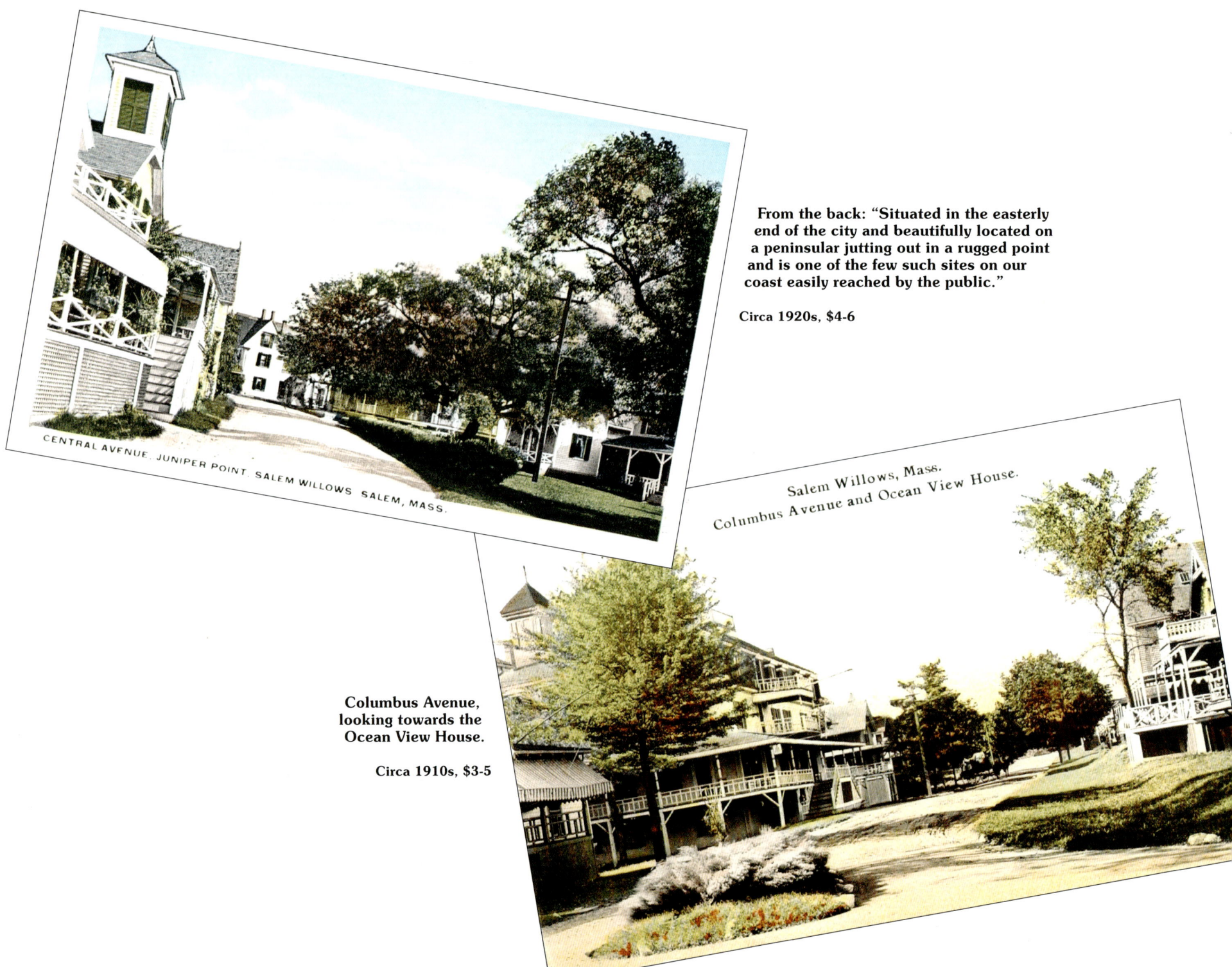

From the back: "Situated in the easterly end of the city and beautifully located on a peninsular jutting out in a rugged point and is one of the few such sites on our coast easily reached by the public."

Circa 1920s, $4-6

Columbus Avenue, looking towards the Ocean View House.

Circa 1910s, $3-5

Juniper Point Beach.

Cancelled 1921, $4-6

Comfortable rooms and an excellent ocean view were both available at the Juniper Point Inn.

Circa 1920s, $4-6

BIBLIOGRAPHY

"Architecture in the 17th and 18th Centuries." *SalemWeb*. http://www.salem-web.com/guide/arch/houses.shtml. 7/18/06.

"Church History and Archives." *First Church in Salem*. http://www.firstchurchinsalem.org/history.htm. 7/17/06.

"Derby Street Historic District." *SalemWeb*. http://www.salemweb.com/guide/arch/ddistrict.shtml. 7/18/06.

Foulke, Patricia and Robert. *Colonial America: A Traveler's Guide*. Old Saybrook: The Globe Pequot Press, 1994.

"Great Salem Fire of 1914." *Wikipedia*. http://en.wikipedia.org/wiki/Great_Salem_Fire_of_1914. 7/17/06.

Hawthorne, Nathaniel. *The House of Seven Gables*. http://www.gutenberg.org/dirs/etext93/77gabl10.txt. 7/17/06.

"Historical Profile." *City of Salem, MA*. http://www.salem.com/Pages/SalemMA_Clerk/historicalprofile. 7/21/06.

"History of the Building." *Salem Public Library*. http://www.noblenet.org/Salem/library/history.html. 7/17/06.

"History of the Building." *Salem Wesley Church*. http://www.salemwesley.org/History.htm. 7/17/06.

"The History of the Catholic Church and Immaculate Conception Parish in Salem, Massachusetts." *Immaculate Conception Parish*. http://www.icsalem.com/history/index.php. 7/17/06.

"The House of Seven Gables." *Wikipedia*. http://en.wikipedia.org/wiki/House_of_Seven_Gables. 7/14/06.

Jones, Arthur B. "Chapter VI – The Conflagration." *The Salem Fire*. http://www.usgennet.org/usa/ma/county/essex/books/fire/set1/chap6.htm. 7/17/06.

"Lafayette Street Historic District." *SalemWeb*. http://www.salemweb.com/guide/arch/ldistrict.shtml. 7/18/06.

"Massachusetts Bay Colony." *Wikipedia*. http://en.wikipedia.org/wiki/Massachusetts_Bay_Company. 7/14/06.

Maynard, Mary. *Dead and Buried in New England: Respectful Visits to the Tombstones and Monuments of 306 Noteworthy Yankees*. Yankee Books, 1993.

McAllister, Jim. "Along the Shoreline: Salem Harbor." *Salem Tales*. http://www.salemweb.com/tales/shoreline.shtml. 7/19/06.

McAllister, Jim. "Baker's Island." *Salem Tales*. http://www.salemweb.com/tales/bakersisland.shtml. 7/19/06.

McAllister, Jim. "Chart(er)ing a Course Through Times Past." *Salem Tales*. http://www.salemweb.com/tales/charter.shtml. 7/17/06.

McAllister, Jim. "East India Marine Hall: Dedicated 1825." *Salem Tales*. http://www.salemweb.com/tales/eastindiamarinehall.shtml. 7/19/06.

McAllister, Jim. "Gathering Places." *Salem Tales*. http://www.salemweb.com/tales/gathering_places.shtml. 7/19/06.

McAllister, Jim. "The Grimshawe House and Elizabeth Peabody." *Salem Tales*. http://www.salemweb.com/tales/grimshawe.shtml. 7/14/06.

McAllister, Jim. "Nathaniel Hawthorne's Neighborhood." *Salem Tales*. http://www.salemweb.com/tales/hawthorne1.shtml. 7/14/06.

McAllister, Jim. "Notable Salem Structures." *Salem Tales*. http://www.salemweb.com/tales/structures.shtml. 7/14/06.

McAllister, Jim. "Pioneer Village: Salem 1630." *Salem Tales*. http://www.salemweb.com/tales/pioneervillage.shtml. 7/14/06.

McAllister, Jim. "Salem Athenaeum: Private Library." *Salem Tales*. http://www.salemweb.com/tales/athenm.shtml. 7/14/06.

McAllister, Jim. "Salem Willows: A Trip to 'The Willows.'" *Salem Tales*. http://www.salemweb.com/tales/willows.shtml. 7/19/06.

McAllister, Jim. "Samuel McIntire: Architect and Carver of Salem (1757-1811)." *Salem Tales*. http://www.salemweb.com/tales/mcintire.shtml. 7/19/06.

"McIntire Historic District." *SalemWeb*. http://www.salemweb.com/guide/arch/mdistrict.shtml. 7/18/06.

National Geographic Society. *New England: Land of Scenic Splendor*. Washington D.C.: National Geographic Society, 1989.

National Park Service. "Nathaniel Hawthorne's Salem: Literary Salem in the Early Nineteenth Century, A Walking Tour." http://www.nps.gov/sama/indepth/pdfs/Text.pdf. 7/17/06.

"Nathaniel Hawthorne." *Wikipedia*. http://en.wikipedia.org/wiki/Nathaniel_Hawthorne. 7/17/06.

Norton, Mary Beth. *In the Devil's Snare: The Salem Witchcraft Crisis of 1692*. New York: Alfred A. Knopf, 2002.

"Peabody Essex Museum." *Wikipedia*. http://en.wikipedia.org/wiki/Peabody_Essex_Museum. 7/19/06.

Perley, Sidney. "The First School." *The History of Salem, Massachusetts*. http://etext.lib.Virginia.edu/salem/witchcraft/Perley/vol2/images/p-291.html. 7/18/06.

"Roger Conant." *Wikipedia*. http://en.wikipedia.org/wiki/Roger_Conant. 7/14/06.

"Salem Common." *SalemWeb*. http://www.salemweb.com/guide/common/. 7/18/06.

"Salem, Massachusetts." *Wikipedia*. http://en.wikipedia.org/wiki/Salem%2C_Massachusetts. 7/14/06.

"Salem State College." *Wikipedia*. http://en.wikipedia.org/wiki/Salem_State_College. 7/18/06.

"Salem Witch Trials." *Wikipedia*. http://en.wikipedia.org/wiki/Salem_Witch_Trials. 7/14/06.

"Washington Square Historic District." *SalemWeb*. http://www.salemweb.com/guide/arch/wdistrict.shtml. 7/18/06.

"Winthrop Fleet." *Wikipedia*. http://en.wikipedia.org/wiki/Winthrop_Fleet. 7/14/06.

INDEX

23rd Regiment Massachusetts Volunteer Infantry Monument 12
Abbott Cove 119
Andrew Safford House, Peabody Essex Museum 109, 110
Arabella 8
Arlington Street 23
Assembly House, Peabody Essex Museum 111

Baker's Island 93, 94
Bertram, Captain John 44, 45
Bertram Home for Aged Men 43
Beverly Bridge 56, 99
Bishop, Bridget 18
Bowdoin House 83
Burgess Point 95
Burying Point 69

Cabot-Endicott House 78, 79
Chase Willow House 122
Charter Street Burying Point 69
Chestnut Street 54, 55, 88
City Hall 37
City Orphan Asylum 44
Cleopatra's Barge 95
Columbus Avenue 124
Conant, Roger 7, 9, 10
Cook Oliver House 81, 82
Corwin, Jonathan 15
Crosby (Nicholas) House 78
Custom House 28, 36

Daniel & Lowe Company 50
Dearborn Street 55
Derby House 81
Derby Wharf 95
Dudley Woodbridge House 83

East Church 67
East India Marine Hall, Peabody Essex Museum 100, 101, 102, 103
Eastern Railroad 41
Ebsen's Willow's House 121
Elias Hasket Derby House 74
Emerton House 86
Emmanuel Downing House 78

Endicott, Jonathan 10, 11
English, Phillip 64, 76
Essex Institute, Peabody Essex Museum 51, 103, 104, 105, 106
Essex Street 51
Ezekiel Hersey Derby House 80

Faire House 11
Fame (Ship) 103
Federal Street 52
First Baptist Church 62
First Church 47, 66
Floating Bridge 56
Forest River 99
Forrester (John) House 82

Gallows Hill 19
Gardner-Pingree House, Peabody Essex Museum 106, 107, 108
Great Salem Fire of 1914 20, 21, 22, 23, 24, 25, 26, 53
Greenlawn Cemetery 68, 69, 70
Grimshawe House 29

Hathorne, John 19
Hathaway House, House of Seven Gables 30, 31, 32, 33, 34, 35
Hawthorne Hotel 97
Hawthorn, Nathaniel 27, 28, 30, 31, 32, 36, 97
Home for Aged Women (Brookehouse for Women) 45
Hosmer-Townsend-Waters House 82
Hotel Lincoln 97

Immaculate Conception Church 62

J. C. B. Memorial 98, 99
J. Howard Fallen House 89
Jacobs, George 16
John Albion Andrew House 89
Juniper Point, Salem Willows 123, 125

Lafayette Street 53, 57
Lee Mansion 84
Lindall family 70

Manning House 28, 90
Masonic Temple 46
Market House 41
Market Place 42
Mather, Nathaniel 70
McIntire Historic District 88
McIntire, Samuel 67, 70, 86
More, Richard 70

Nathaniel Hawthorne Birthplace 28
Cotton Company 71, 72
Nichols House 90
North Bridge 104
North Church 66
North Shore Babies Hospital 44
North Shore Garden 98

Old Lord Estate 91
Old North Bridge 56
Osgood Hydrangea Garden 91

Peabody Essex Museum 40
Peirce-Nichols House 111, 112
Pequot House 75, 76
Pequot Mills 72
Phenix Hall 41
Phillips School 58
Pickering House 77
Pickering Street 87
Pickman-Shreve-Little House 85
Pineapple Doorway 83
Plummer Hall 106
Poor Estate 74
Probate Court House 39

Retire Beckett House, House of Seven Gables 35
Ropes Mansion, Peabody Essex Museum 112, 113, 114, 115

Salem Athenaeum 42
Salem Common 7, 25, 48, 49
Salem Club 42, 91
Salem Harbor 120
Salem High School 58, 59
Salem Hospital 43

Salem Mansion 73
Salem Pentecostal Church 62
Salem Pioneer Village 9
Salem Public Library 39, 40
Salem Willows 116, 117, 118, 119, 120, 121, 122, 123, 124, 125
Salem Willows Yacht Club 119
Salem Witch Museum 19
Salem Witch Trials 13, 17, 18, 39
Saltonstall, Leverett 84
Saltonstall School 57
Scarlet Letter House 29
Shattuck Witch House 15
Shreve House 85
South Church (First Church) 67
South Congregational Church 61
St. James School 60
St. Joseph's Church 25, 64, 65
St. Peter's Church 63
State Normal School (Salem State College) 59, 60
Story, Joseph (Judge) 81
Superior Court House 37, 39
Swenbeck's 122

Town House Square 47
Tucker Rice House 88

United Methodist Church 63

Ward, John 109
Washington Square (Salem Common) 48, 49
Washington Street 47, 52
Wesley Methodist Episcopal Church (Wesley United Methodist Church) 63
White (Captain Joseph) 107
Winter Island 94
Winthrop, John 8, 9
Whipple (George M.) House 74, 84
Witch House 15, 16
Witch Jail 17

Y. M. C. A. 46
Y. W. C. A. 46